1,000 FACTS ABOUT SPACE

DEAN REGAS

Westerlund 2: a giant
cluster of 3,000 stars

TABLE OF CONTENTS

Four of the galaxies in Stephan's Quintet—a group of five galaxies inside the constellation Pegasus

6

When I was a kid, I loved to see the pictures of the planets taken by space missions, the videos of astronauts bounding across the moon, and the mysterious views telescopes shared of galaxies far, far away. Although you and I may not be able to travel in space yet, our imaginations can soar, and the facts in this book are your ticket to outer space. Your destination: anywhere in the universe.

I am an astronomer who works at the Cincinnati Observatory. My job is to study outer space—as much of it as I can. I use telescopes to look at the moon, stars, planets, asteroids, comets, star clusters, nebulae, galaxies, and even the sun (with proper professional solar filters).

There is just so much of the universe to study, and I cannot see it all. Astronomers around the world are just as curious as I am. And every day they discover something new. Every day they find new asteroids, stars, and galaxies. And that means every day I get to go to work and learn something new.

In fact, I even have an asteroid named after me: 8815 Deanregas!

In this book you can see some of the amazing sights I've seen in telescopes—plus a lot more that are spread out across all of space. You'll learn about what it's like to live in space and to walk on the moon. You'll explore the rings of Saturn, check out the strangest stars in our galaxy, and dive into a black hole. You'll travel to alien worlds that have several suns in their skies and start counting the billions and billions of galaxies in our universe.

The facts in this book are laid out so you can flip to any page and learn something new. If you especially like a certain part of the universe, you can go to that section and read and reread it until you know all about it. I hope you find a lot of facts in here that you can share with others.

So sit back, get in launch position, and prepare to blast off on a journey to the farthest reaches of the universe.

Dean Regas
Astronomer, Cincinnati Observatory

Astronomer Dean Regas

10 ASTRONOMICALLY HUGE

1

NOTHING IS BIGGER THAN **THE UNIVERSE.** THE UNIVERSE IS ALL THE STARS, PLANETS, GALAXIES, GASES, MASSES, AND EVERYTHING THAT EVER WAS OR EVER WILL BE.

3

The **LARGEST KNOWN STAR** may be a red supergiant named **UY SCUTI.** It is about **3.69 BILLION TIMES LARGER THAN OUR SUN.**

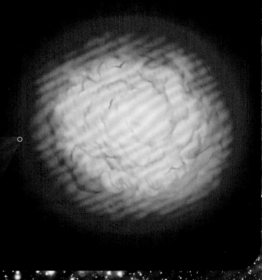

2

Astronomers believe the universe began about **13.8 BILLION YEARS AGO.** All matter exploded outward from one tiny point, called a SINGULARITY. That explosion was the **BIG BANG.**

4

When a supermassive (extremely big) star explodes, it's called a **SUPERNOVA.** A supernova can create more light in one moment than an **ENTIRE GALAXY OF BILLIONS OF STARS** does.

5

THE **BRIGHTEST SUPERNOVA EVER RECORDED** was seen on May 1, 1006. A star suddenly flared up and for a short time was **ALMOST AS BRIGHT IN THE SKY AS THE MOON.**

FACTS ABOUT THE UNIVERSE

6

In 2019, a team of astronomers from around the world worked together to capture the FIRST EVER PICTURE OF A **BLACK HOLE.** The huge black hole, called M87*, lies at the heart of a massive galaxy and weighs as much as **6.5 BILLION SUNS.**

7

The brightest events that astronomers ever see are called **GAMMA-RAY BURSTS.** These appear when a star shoots out as much energy in a few seconds as our sun does in 10 BILLION YEARS.

8

From November 12 to 13, 1833, the BIGGEST METEOR STORM in modern history struck Earth. Between 100,000 and 240,000 meteors were seen streaking across the sky that night and into the next morning.

9

IN JULY 1994, COMET SHOEMAKER-LEVY 9 BROKE INTO DOZENS OF PIECES AND CRASHED INTO JUPITER. IT WAS THE BIGGEST COLLISION EVER SEEN IN OUR SOLAR SYSTEM. ONE PIECE OF COMET LEFT A DARK SCAR ON JUPITER **BIGGER THAN EARTH.**

10

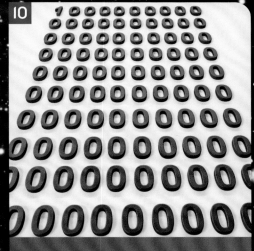

Some evidence suggests that the universe could exist for another **one GOOGOL years** (that's a one, followed by 100 zeros).

Carina Nebula

❶ Our solar system is made up of the sun and all the objects that circle around it. They include planets, moons, dwarf planets, asteroids, comets, Centaurs, Trojans, and cubewanos.

❷ Most scientists believe that our solar system began 4.6 billion years ago as a huge cloud of gas and dust called a nebula.

❸ Astronomers have observed one star (the sun), eight planets, five dwarf planets, more than 200 moons, more than 900,000 asteroids, and more than 3,600 comets in our solar system.

❹ Our solar system started when the largest portion of the nebula formed into the sun. Around it, swirling gases and materials formed into planets, asteroids, and other objects.

❺ The solar system can be broken down into sections: inner planets, asteroid belt, outer planets, Kuiper belt, and Oort cloud.

❻ The inner planets (Mercury, Venus, Earth, and Mars) are made mostly of rock. That was the only material that could survive the heat and pressure so close to the newly formed sun.

❼ Ices, liquids, and gases were pushed to the cooler outer solar system. There, gravity brought them together to form the large outer planets: Jupiter, Saturn, Uranus, and Neptune.

OUR SOLAR SYSTEM

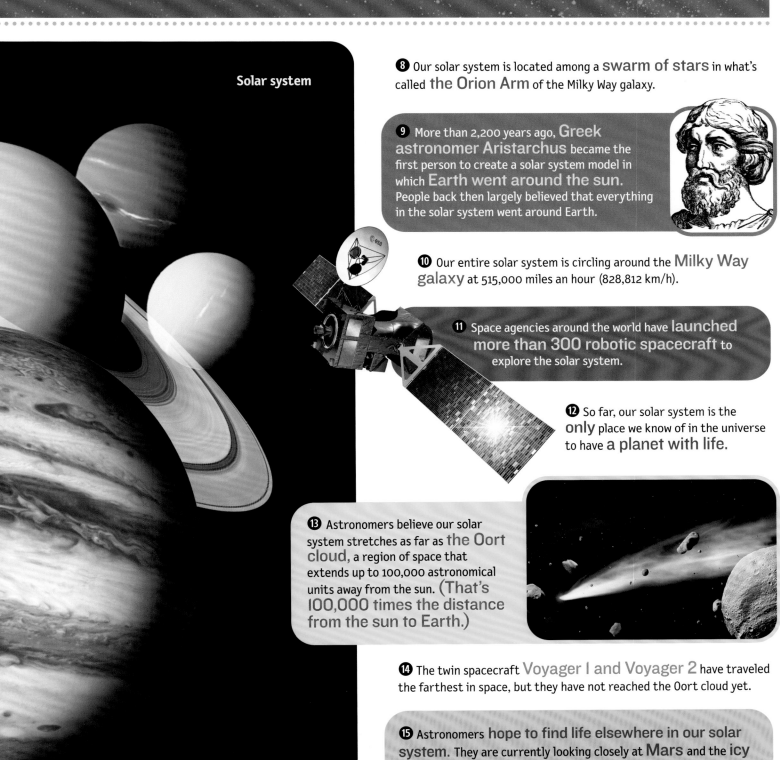

Solar system

8 Our solar system is located among a swarm of stars in what's called the Orion Arm of the Milky Way galaxy.

9 More than 2,200 years ago, Greek astronomer Aristarchus became the first person to create a solar system model in which Earth went around the sun. People back then largely believed that everything in the solar system went around Earth.

10 Our entire solar system is circling around the Milky Way galaxy at 515,000 miles an hour (828,812 km/h).

11 Space agencies around the world have launched more than 300 robotic spacecraft to explore the solar system.

12 So far, our solar system is the only place we know of in the universe to have a planet with life.

13 Astronomers believe our solar system stretches as far as the Oort cloud, a region of space that extends up to 100,000 astronomical units away from the sun. (That's 100,000 times the distance from the sun to Earth.)

14 The twin spacecraft Voyager 1 and Voyager 2 have traveled the farthest in space, but they have not reached the Oort cloud yet.

15 Astronomers hope to find life elsewhere in our solar system. They are currently looking closely at Mars and the icy moons Europa and Enceladus for signs of living things.

15 QUICK FACTS ABOUT

APRIL 15

❶ Our concept of time—how we mark days, months, years, and more—comes from astronomers noting patterns in the movement of the sun, moon, and stars.

❷ Earth has two kinds of days. A sidereal day on Earth is 23 hours and 56 minutes long. This is how long it takes for Earth to spin completely around on its axis once.

❸ A solar day is the time it takes for a spot on Earth to spin around to face the sun again. At 24 hours, it is longer than a sidereal day. That's because Earth is moving in space while it spins.

❹ Ancient scholars named the seven days of the week after the seven bright objects that move regularly through the constellations: sun, moon, Mars, Mercury, Jupiter, Venus, and Saturn.

❺ Sunday is the "Sun's Day," Monday is the "Moon's Day," and Saturday is "Saturn's Day."

❻ The names Tuesday, Wednesday, Thursday, and Friday come from Norse mythology and its gods, linked to the planets Mars, Mercury, Jupiter, and Venus.

❼ It takes the moon about 29.5 days to complete a full cycle of its phases. Astronomers call this a synodic month. Sometimes they give it the nickname "moonth."

Star trails over the Himalaya

MEASURING TIME

8 Nineteen years from now, **the moon will look the same and be in about the same place** as you see it tonight. Greek astronomer Meton figured out this pattern more than 2,400 years ago.

9 A **year** is the time it takes Earth to complete one trip—**one orbit**—around the sun. It equals **365 days, five hours, 48 minutes, and 46 seconds.**

10 Because it doesn't take **exactly 365 days** to complete a year, astronomers **add a leap day every four years** (February 29) to balance out the calendar.

11 The entire solar system is circling the center of the Milky Way galaxy. **A galactic year** is the time it takes the sun and planets to complete one orbit around the center— **about 230 million Earth years.**

12 The **oldest rocks on Earth** have helped scientists estimate the age of our planet: It's about **4.54 billion years old.**

13 Our sun formed about **4.6 billion years ago,** but some **stars** you see at night could be **two or three times older.**

14 Modern **cosmologists**—scientists who study the beginning of the universe—believe the universe we live in began **13.8 billion years ago.**

15 In the early 20th century, physicist Albert Einstein showed that **space and time were linked.** The **Inca of Peru** had a word, *pacha,* that connected those two key astronomical concepts **hundreds of years before Einstein did.**

1
Our sun is a **star,** a ball of gas that creates its own light and heat in its **fiery core.**

2
All the planets, asteroids, and comets in our solar system **circle around the sun.**

3
The enormous sun holds **99.8 percent of the mass** of our solar system. The planets, moons, asteroids, and comets make up **0.2 percent.**

4
The sun formed from a giant cloud of gas and dust, called **a nebula,** about 4.6 billion years ago. It will exist for another five billion more.

5
The **distance from the sun to Earth** changes over the course of a year from 91 million miles to 94 million miles (146 million km to 151 million km). The average distance is about **93 million miles (150 million km).**

6
The sun is **eight light-minutes away.** That means it takes light eight minutes to travel **from the sun to Earth.**

7
The sun is huge! Its **diameter** (width) is about 865,000 miles (1,392,000 km). You could fit **109 Earths, side to side,** across the width of the sun.

8
The sun is **much larger** than all the planets put together. In fact, you could fit **1,300,000 Earths** inside the sun and still have room for Pluto.

9
Although other bodies, including planets, can be a little squished, the sun is almost **perfectly round.** The sun is the most **spherical,** or ball-like, object in the solar system.

10
The sun is made up almost entirely of **hydrogen and helium** gases. It has other elements, too, but they make up less **than one percent** of its volume.

11
Different parts of the sun spin at different speeds. It takes about **25 days** for the sun's center to spin around once. At the poles, it takes about **36 days.**

12
The **hottest part** of the sun is the center, called the **core.** There, temperatures may reach **27,000,000°F (15,000,000°C).**

13
The **outer layer** of the sun, the ball of light you see from Earth, is called the **photosphere.**

14
Our yellow-white sun is about **10,000°F (5538°C)** on its **surface.**

15
Do not stare at the sun with your naked eye or through a telescope. It is so bright that it could hurt your eyes or even **blind you.**

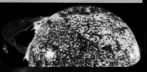

16
You can safely observe the sun only by using **proper solar filters.** Specially made eclipse shades have lenses dark enough to look at the sun without damaging your eyes.

17
Dark sunspots often pepper the surface of the sun. They are the sites of huge **eruptions of gas.**

18
Sunspots show up as darker spots because they are **slightly cooler** than the gas around them. While the surface of the sun is about 10,000°F (5538°C), sunspots can be as cool as 7200°F (3982°C). **That's still hot!**

19
Even a small sunspot is still thousands of miles wide. Many sunspots you see in pictures are **larger than Earth.**

20
Every 11 years the sun has a lot of sunspots during a time called **solar maximum.** Astronomers call the times of few sunspots **solar minimum.**

21
Astronomers **cannot predict** where sunspots will pop up or how long they will last. Some sunspots last a few hours, while others hang around for **a month.**

22
The sun is **explosive.** Violent eruptions called **prominences, flares, and coronal mass ejections** blast off the sun almost daily.

23
Solar prominences often **look like loops.** They happen when gases shoot off the surface of the sun, cool off, and then fall back to the sun again.

24
Solar flares are **violent explosions** of material that burst from the **sun's surface** in a matter of minutes.

25
Coronal mass ejections (CMEs) are the **most powerful solar explosions.** They shoot superhot gases off the sun and into space at around 1.2 million miles an hour (1.9 million km/h).

26
Even at more than a **million miles an hour,** it still takes CMEs **three days** to travel the 93 million miles (150 million km) to Earth.

27
When a CME runs into Earth, you are safe on the ground. **Its gases get trapped** high in the atmosphere.

28
Above the sun's photosphere is a layer called the **chromosphere.** Here, gases cool to around 7700°F (4260°C).

29
The only time you can see the chromosphere from Earth is during **a total solar eclipse—**when the moon blocks out most of the sun.

30
Above the chromosphere is the **corona,** the outer layer of the sun.

31
Even though the corona is farther from the sun's core than the photosphere or chromosphere, it is way hotter than those layers. In fact, the corona can be 2,000,000°F (1,100,000°C) or more!

32
Astronomers are still trying to understand why the corona is so hot.

33
We learn a lot about the sun from unpiloted spacecraft. For instance, the Solar and Heliospheric Observatory (SOHO) has circled the sun for more than 25 years, taking amazing images and videos of our star.

34
From Earth, we can see only one side of the sun at any time. NASA sent twin space probes, called STEREO, to the sun so astronomers could see two different parts at once.

35
The Solar Dynamics Observatory spacecraft watches the sun closely for changes in its surface. It has taken videos of giant eruptions shooting off into space.

36
NASA launched the spacecraft Genesis in 2001 to collect pieces of solar wind (particles shot out from the sun). When it returned to Earth, it accidentally crashed, but astronomers were still able to save some of the solar material.

37
The Parker Solar Probe orbits the sun to study its extremely hot corona. It swings close to the sun's surface, facing more heat than any other spacecraft.

38
The Ulysses spacecraft circled around the north and south poles of the sun to view parts of the solar surface not easily seen from Earth.

39
When the sun begins to run out of fuel, in about four to five billion years, it will get larger and larger and turn orange, then red.

40
In about five billion years, the sun will be a red giant star. It will swallow up Mercury and Venus and may even engulf Earth.

41
At the end of its existence, the sun will not be able to hold itself together. Its outer layers will fly off into space, creating a ring of gas called a planetary nebula.

42
After the sun becomes a planetary nebula, a tiny white star will be left behind. Our old sun will be changed into a new star called a white dwarf.

43
The new sun, now a white dwarf, could live on for billions or even trillions of years.

44
Only three large objects in space regularly come between Earth and the sun: the moon during a solar eclipse, and the planets Venus (here in a time-lapse photo) and Mercury in events called transits.

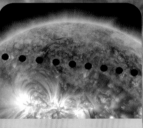

45
Earth is closest to the sun around every January 4. It is farthest from the sun around every July 4.

46
Earth's four seasons are caused by the planet's tilt as we travel around the sun—not by the distance to the sun.

47
The summer solstice, also known as the first day of summer, is the day when we have the most hours of daylight and the fewest hours of darkness.

48
The winter solstice, also known as the first day of winter, is the day when we have the fewest hours of daylight and the most hours of darkness.

49
On the spring and fall equinoxes, the entire Earth has 12 hours of daylight and 12 hours of darkness.

50
Hawaii is the only state in the United States where the sun can appear straight overhead in the sky.

50 SHINING Facts About THE SUN

Sunspots on the sun's surface

15 MINIATURE FACTS

1 Mercury is the **closest planet to the sun.** Its orbit takes it **as close as 30 million miles** (48 million km) to about **43 million miles** (69 million km) at its farthest point.

2 At only 3,032 miles (4,880 km) in diameter, Mercury is **the smallest planet in the solar system.**

3 **Daytime temperatures on Mercury** reach a sizzling **800°F** (427°C), hot enough to melt lead. But once the sun sets, the temperature **plummets to minus 279°F** (-173°C), three times colder than the South Pole on Earth.

4 Although Mercury is closest to the sun, **it is not the hottest planet.** Wrapped in its blanket of clouds, **Venus is slightly warmer** than Mercury.

5 **If you were standing on Mercury,** on certain days the sun would look **nine times larger** and shine **nine times brighter** than it does from Earth.

6 Of all the planets in our solar system, **Mercury is the darkest color.** It is about the same color as blacktop or the pavement of a **well-traveled highway.**

7 As hot as it is, **Mercury has ice.** The sun never reaches **deep down in craters** at the north and south poles of Mercury. Astronomers have found frozen water there.

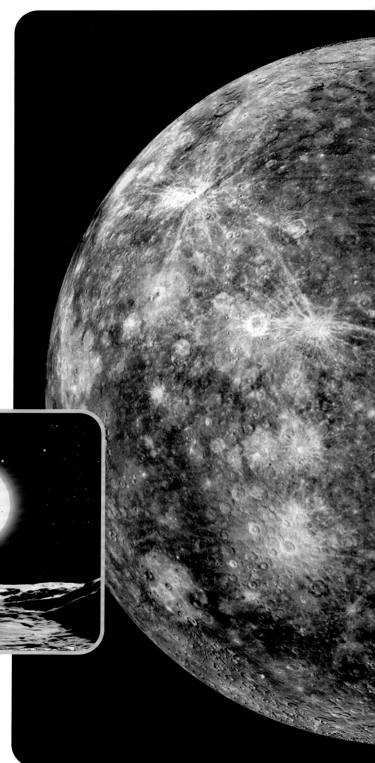

ABOUT MERCURY

Mercury

8 Mercury is **covered in craters** made by meteors and asteroids hitting the surface a long time ago. **The biggest, Caloris Basin,** is larger than Texas, U.S.A.

9 Mercury's **gravity** is 38 percent as strong as Earth's. So if you weigh 100 pounds (45 kg) on Earth, you'd weigh **only 38 pounds (17 kg)** on Mercury.

10 Mercury is by far **the fastest planet** in the solar system. It travels at an average of almost **106,000 miles an hour (170,590 km/h)** in its path around the sun.

11 Mercury takes only 88 Earth days to circle the sun. If you lived there, **you'd have a birthday every 88 days!**

12 Because Mercury spins so slowly and travels around the sun so quickly, in some places and at some times in a Mercury year, **you could see the sun rise, stop, and set again in the same place.**

13 Mercury is the **toughest planet to see from Earth,** because it is always near the bright sun in the sky. You can see it only occasionally before sunrise or after sunset.

14 Mercury **doesn't have any moons** circling it.

15 The **MESSENGER spacecraft** circled Mercury and made **the first map of the entire planet.** Then it crashed—on purpose—into its surface.

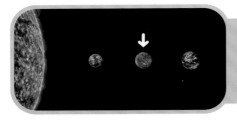

1 Venus is the **second closest planet** to the sun. It orbits our star at a distance of about **66 million miles** (106 million km).

2 Venus is 7,521 miles (12,104 km) wide. That makes it the planet **closest in size to Earth.** It is sometimes called our **sister planet.**

3 The **gravity on Venus** is 90 percent that of Earth. So if you weighed 100 pounds (45 kg) on Earth, **you'd weigh only 90 pounds** (41 kg) on Venus.

4 Venus is **blanketed by a thick atmosphere** that traps heat from the sun like a greenhouse. That's why it's **hotter than Mercury** and has a constant temperature across the entire planet.

5 The **weather on Venus** is easy to predict. Every day, everywhere, daytime or nighttime, summer or winter, **it is cloudy and hot, hot, hot:** 864°F (462°C).

6 The **weight of Venus's dense atmosphere** is so intense that if you stood on the planet, even in a space suit, your body would not be able to withstand it.

7 Venus's **surface is rocky,** with mountains, valleys, craters, and the **remains of ancient volcanoes.**

COVERED VENUS

Venus

8 A day on Venus is longer than its year. Although it takes Venus 225 Earth days to circle the sun, it spins so slowly that it takes 243 Earth days to rotate one time.

9 Venus is the most tilted planet in our solar system. Earth is tilted 23.5 degrees; Venus is basically tipped upside down, and it spins backward compared to Earth.

10 Like Mercury, Venus has no moons.

11 Venus is a planet, but it is sometimes known as the evening or morning star because you see Venus in the sky just after sunset or just before sunrise.

12 From Earth, Venus is the brightest starlike object in the sky. In fact, it is so suspiciously bright that many people mistake it for a UFO.

13 It's been hard for humans to explore Venus! Twelve of the first 13 space missions sent to the planet failed during launch, on the way, or when trying to land.

14 For a long time, astronomers did not know what Venus looked like under its thick atmosphere. Then the Magellan spacecraft circled the planet and used radar to map its surface, creating the first global map of our sister planet.

15 The Venera 13 mission, a robotic spacecraft launched in 1981 by the Soviet Union, has the record for surviving the longest on Venus before being crushed and melted by the harsh conditions: just 127 minutes.

❶ Earth is your **home planet.** It is the planet where you and everyone you know lives.

❷ Earth is the **third planet from the sun.** It circles our star at an average distance of **93 million miles** (150 million km).

3 Sometimes astronomers refer to Earth as **a "Goldilocks planet,"** because it is not too close to the sun (and too hot) and not too far from the sun (and too cold) to support life.

❹ At the Equator, Earth spins at about 1,000 miles an hour (1,600 km/h). The farther north or south you go from the Equator, the slower Earth spins each day.

❺ **Earth's rotation causes day and night.** When you are pointing toward the sun, it is **daytime.** When you spin away from the sun, it is **nighttime.**

❻ Because Earth is **tilted by 23.5 degrees** as it circles the sun, our planet experiences **four seasons.** Each lasts about three months.

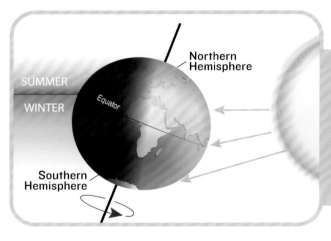

Northern Hemisphere

SUMMER

WINTER

Equator

Southern Hemisphere

❼ When Earth's **Northern Hemisphere** is tilted toward the sun, people there have **summer.** At the same time, the **Southern Hemisphere** is tilted away from the sun, and people there experience **winter.**

ABOUT EARTH

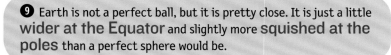

Earth

8 At 7,918 miles (12,743 km) wide, Earth is the largest and most massive of the rocky planets in our solar system— bigger than Mercury, Venus, or Mars.

9 Earth is not a perfect ball, but it is pretty close. It is just a little wider at the Equator and slightly more squished at the poles than a perfect sphere would be.

10 Earth is the only place we know that has an atmosphere we can breathe. Our air is 78 percent nitrogen, 21 percent oxygen, and one percent other elements. Perfect for us!

11 If you could put Earth on a huge scale, it would weigh 13 septillion pounds (6 septillion kg).

12 Earth is the only planet not named after a Greek or Roman god or goddess. The name comes from a Germanic word that means "ground."

13 More than two-thirds—about 70 percent—of Earth's surface is covered by water. This vast region includes the Pacific, Atlantic, Indian, Southern, and Arctic Oceans.

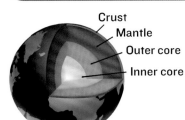

Crust
Mantle
Outer core
Inner core

14 From deep inside to the surface, Earth has four main layers of rock: the inner core, outer core, mantle, and crust.

15 The inner core of Earth is about 759 miles (1,221 km) wide and is made mostly of the metals iron and nickel. Electric currents in the liquid metal create a magnetic field around Earth.

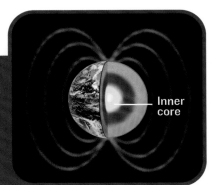

Inner core

1
Other than the occasional passing asteroid and artificial satellites, the moon is **Earth's closest neighbor in space.** It orbits our planet at an average distance of 238,855 miles (384,400 km).

2
Because it orbits Earth, the moon is also called Earth's **natural satellite.**

3
The moon is the **largest and brightest** object in the nighttime sky.

4
The moon's distance from our planet constantly changes. When the moon is closest to Earth, at about 225,000 miles (363,300 km), astronomers call that **perigee.**

5
When the moon is **farthest** from Earth, at almost 252,000 miles (406,000 km), that is called **apogee.**

6
The moon is 2,159 miles (3,475 km) in diameter. If you put the moon next to Earth, it is only a little more than one-fourth Earth's diameter— **roughly the size of a tennis ball compared to a basketball.**

7
The **force of gravity** on the moon is about one-sixth that of Earth. If you weigh 100 pounds (45 kg) on Earth, **you would weigh only 17 pounds (8 kg)** on the moon.

8
Our moon is the **fifth largest natural satellite** in the solar system. Only Jupiter's moons Ganymede, Callisto, and Io and Saturn's moon Titan are bigger than ours.

9
The moon is made of **rock.** The surface is covered by dark gray boulders, pebbles, and dust called **lunar regolith.**

10
The full moon closest to Earth in a calendar year is known as a **supermoon.** A supermoon is **14 percent larger and 30 percent brighter** than the farthest full moon (sometimes called a puny moon).

11
Astronomers **don't use the term "supermoon."** They have a scientific name: **perigee-syzygy** (PAIR-uh-jee SIH-zuh-jee).

12
The moon **used to be closer to Earth.** It moves about an inch (2.5 cm) farther away every year.

13
The pull of **the moon's gravity** is the main reason Earth has **tides**— the twice-daily rise and fall of sea levels.

14
People from different cultures see different shapes on the moon's shadowy surface. Some see a **"man in the moon"** and others a **"rabbit in the moon."**

15
The moon **makes no light of its own.** It shines with **reflected sunlight.** The sun lights up half the moon at one time.

16
The lighted side of the moon **seems to change shape in the sky** from night to night.

17
These **phases** are called new moon (when it is all dark), waxing crescent, first quarter, waxing gibbous, full moon, waning gibbous, third quarter, and waning crescent.

18
Every time **a full moon rises,** the sun sets on the opposite side of the sky **at the same time.** The full moon also sets just as the sun rises the following morning.

19
It takes about **29.5 days** for the moon to go through one complete cycle of phases. This is called a **synodic month.**

20
The only time you can see a **new moon** is during a **solar eclipse.** During these rare events, you can (with special protective eclipse glasses) see the new moon outlined in front of the sun.

21
From Earth, the moon looks bigger to us when it is near the horizon. This effect is called **the moon illusion.**

50 MAGNIFICENT Facts About THE MOON

22
If you visited the moon, you would see Earth go through phases. You would see a **new Earth** grow into a crescent Earth, gibbous Earth, and full Earth and then shrink again.

23
From the moon, **Earth looks four times wider and 16 times larger** than the moon does from Earth.

24
Astronomers call the side of the moon you can see the **near side.** The side you never see is the **far side.**

25
A full day on the moon lasts **29.5 Earth days.** So when the sun sets, it is dark for half that time: almost 15 straight Earth days.

26
A "blue moon" is the second full moon in a calendar month. If you have a full moon on October 1, for example, a second full moon on October 31 would be a blue moon.

27
The moon can truly appear blue on rare occasions. **Volcanic eruptions on Earth** that send dust and ash high into the air **change the color of moonlight in the atmosphere.**

28
Many Native American cultures have named the full moons that occur each month. The names include **Wolf Moon** (January), **Worm Moon** (March), and **Hunter's Moon** (October).

29
The **harvest moon** is traditionally the full moon **closest to the north's autumnal equinox** (September 22 or 23). Farmers use its light to help harvest the crops by night.

30
A ring of light around the moon is called a **lunar halo.** It occurs when moonlight bends through lots of six-sided **ice crystals** in Earth's atmosphere.

31
During a full moon, moonlight can reflect off mist from a waterfall and create **a moonbow—a rainbow caused by moonlight.**

32
Most astronomers believe the moon was made **after a huge object struck Earth a long time ago.** The debris from this impact blasted off Earth and eventually formed into the moon.

33
A **full moon** is so bright from reflected sunlight that it is difficult to see details even through a telescope.

34
There are so many **craters** on the moon that they are hard to count. They were **made by asteroids, meteors, and comets** slamming into the lunar surface long ago.

35
Because the moon has **no wind or water** to wear down its surface, its craters have remained **the same** for millions or billions of years.

36
Two large craters named **Copernicus and Kepler** have steep, circular walls. When the moon is nearly full, **they shine** like two bright dots on the lunar surface.

37
The crater named Tycho is 52 miles (84 km) wide. **Streaks of bright rocks named rays** spread outward from Tycho in all directions.

38
In the center of some of the larger craters are **tall, steep mountains.** These central peaks were formed after huge meteors crashed into those sites.

Full moon

39
The line dividing day from night on the moon is called **the terminator.** The terminator is the best place to scan with a telescope and see details on lunar mountains and valleys.

40
There are two main kinds of land on the moon: brighter areas, called **the highlands,** and darker areas, called the seas, or **maria** (MAH-ree-uh).

41
Maria (the moon's seas) are mostly round. They aren't really seas. **They are giant craters** that were partially filled with **lava.**

42
As the moon orbits Earth, **only one side faces our planet,** so unless you leave Earth, you can never see the other side.

43
The moon rotates one time for every revolution it makes around Earth. This is called **synchronous rotation.** It's common among moons in the solar system.

44
If you were standing on the **near side** of the moon, you would always see Earth in the sky.

45
The far side of the moon has **greater numbers of smaller craters** and fewer large, dark seas (or maria) than the near side.

46
The former **Soviet Union** named many of the large features on the far side of the moon, because their robotic craft **were the first to see this side.**

47
The tallest mountain on the moon is named **Mons Huygens.** It is about 18,046 feet (5,500 m) high, about two-thirds as tall as Mount Everest on Earth.

48
Deep in craters near the **south pole** of the moon, where the sun never shines, astronomers have found **frozen water.**

49
The maria (or seas) of the moon include names such as **Sea of Tranquility, Sea of Serenity, Sea of Crises,** and **Sea of Cold.**

50
Many of the mountain ranges on the moon are named after mountains on Earth, such as the **Apennines, Caucasus,** and **Alps.**

1

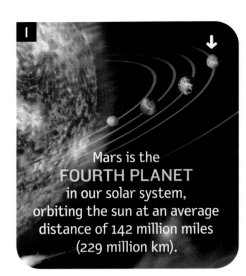

Mars is the
FOURTH PLANET
in our solar system,
orbiting the sun at an average
distance of 142 million miles
(229 million km).

2

Mars is small, just
4,212 miles (6,779 km) in diameter—a
little over **half the width of Earth.**
However, both planets have about the
same amount of dry land.

3

The **gravity** on Mars is
38 percent that of Earth.
So if you weigh 100 pounds (45 kg)
on Earth, you would weigh only
38 pounds (17 kg) on Mars.

4

A day on Mars
is slightly longer than a day on
Earth. It takes Mars
**24 hours,
37 minutes,
and 22
seconds**
to spin once.

5

Of all the planets in the
solar system, Mars is
the most like Earth in
its **TILT**. It tips on its axis
by 25 degrees, compared
to Earth's 23.5.

25 EXPLORATORY FACTS ABOUT

6

Its tilt gives Mars
FOUR SEASONS, just like Earth.
But a year on Mars is **687 EARTH
DAYS,** so each Martian season
lasts almost twice as long
as a season on Earth.

7

MARS LOOKS RED BECAUSE ITS SOIL AND ROCKS ARE
RICH IN **IRON,** AND THEY HAVE **RUSTED** OVER THE YEARS.

8

Mars is known as
THE RED PLANET,
but its color in our sky changes to
**golden, orange, brown, or
pink** based on Earth's cloud cover
and the weather on Mars.

9

Mars has **ice caps** at
its north and south poles that are
made mostly of **water ice.**

10

There are
NO RIVERS OR STREAMS
on the surface of Mars.
The atmosphere is so thin that any
**melted ice or liquid turns
instantly into a gas.**

11

Mars is **extremely dry** now,
but it used to have **great seas
of liquid water and rivers**
that flowed through ravines.

12

As Earth and Mars orbit
the sun, the distance between
them varies a lot. In 2003, Mars
was as close as about 34.6
million miles (55.7 million km).
It won't get closer than that
until the year 2287.

13

The Martian
volcano **Olympus
Mons** is the largest
mountain on any
planet in the solar
system. It is **three
times taller
than Earth's
highest peak,
Mount Everest.**

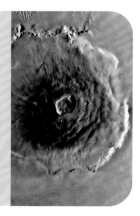

14 Mars has the **longest canyon in the solar system:** Valles Marineris. At more than 2,500 miles (4,023 km) long, 120 miles (193 km) wide, and 7 miles (11 km) deep, **Valles Marineris** looks like a deep gash across the surface of the red planet.

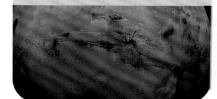

15 The average temperature on Mars is minus 80°F (-62°C), **colder than Earth's South Pole in winter.** The highest temperature recorded on Mars was 86°F (30°C), but the lowest was **minus 284°F** (-176°C).

16 **You cannot breathe the air on Mars.** Mars's atmosphere is only one percent as thick as Earth's and is mostly made of **carbon dioxide.**

17 During the day, the Martian sky looks **pink**, but when the sun sets, **the sky turns BLUE.**

18 MARS PRODUCES **THE LARGEST DUST STORMS** IN THE SOLAR SYSTEM. SOME CAN COVER HALF THE PLANET.

MARS

19 THE RED PLANET HAS **dust devils.** THESE MINI-TORNADOES CAN SWIRL **for miles** ACROSS THE DRY, DESERT LANDSCAPE.

20 Mars has two moons: **PHOBOS AND DEIMOS.** The word *phobos* means "fear," and *deimos* means "dread."

21 Mars's moons are not perfectly round, and **they are only the size of small cities.** Phobos measures about 14 miles (23 km) across, while Deimos is only 8 miles (13 km) wide.

22 In Norse mythology, the god **Tiw** represented Mars. The English word **"Tuesday"** comes from **"Tiw's Day,"** traditionally Mars's day of the week.

23 On July 14, 1965, the American spacecraft MARINER 4 flew about 6,000 miles (almost 10,000 km) above the Martian surface and sent back **the first close-up pictures** of the planet.

24 Mars has had the **most robotic visitors** of any planet beyond Earth. The **Mars Reconnaissance Orbiter** and MAVEN, for example, can see tiny details on the surface from orbit high above.

25 The largest Mars rover, Perseverance, landed on the red planet in 2021. The size of a small car, it is exploring an area once covered by a lake of water.

15 ASTEROID FACTS

❶ Asteroids are small rocky objects that orbit the sun but are not considered planets or moons.

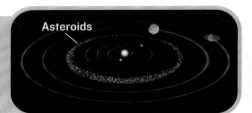
Asteroids

❷ Most of the asteroids in our solar system circle the sun between the orbits of Mars and Jupiter. This area is called the asteroid belt.

❸ New asteroids are discovered every day. Astronomers have found more than 970,000 so far.

❹ Asteroids are pieces of a small planet that never formed. Jupiter's massive gravity kept them scattered in a widespread belt of rocks.

❺ Asteroids come in all shapes and sizes. Some are so small that they look like a pile of rubble barely held together by their weak gravity.

❻ Italian astronomer Giuseppe Piazzi discovered the first asteroid on January 1, 1801. He named it Ceres after the ancient Roman harvest goddess. In 2006, astronomers also named it a dwarf planet.

❼ The tallest mountain in the solar system may be on the asteroid Vesta. Rising 14 miles (23 km) above the surrounding plain, this lofty peak is equal to—or slightly taller than—Olympus Mons, the largest mountain on Mars.

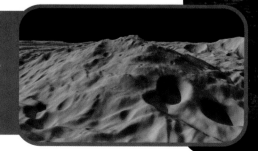
Leonid meteor shower

THAT ROCK

8 In 2011, **NASA's Dawn** spacecraft orbited **Vesta**, then flew over to take a closer look at **Ceres** in 2015—completing a tour of the two largest and roundest asteroids.

9 More than 150 asteroids have their own moons. Asteroid Sylvia has two: **Remus and Romulus.**

10 The space rock named 2015 TC25 is the smallest asteroid ever observed. Astronomers saw this six-foot (2-m)-wide boulder when it flew near Earth in October 2015.

11 **Gravity** on the tiny asteroid **Eros** is very weak. A person weighing 100 pounds (45 kg) on Earth would weigh only an ounce (28 g) on Eros.

12 Astronomers believe an asteroid struck Earth about 65 million years ago. The huge impact changed our planet and led to the extinction of many creatures, including most dinosaurs.

13 Asteroids that take paths closer to our planet are called near-Earth asteroids. Astronomers watch these very closely to make sure none of the larger ones will hit Earth.

14 Many asteroids are named after famous people. For instance: 2309 Mr. Spock, 12818 Tomhanks, 241528 Tubman (for Harriet Tubman), and 5535 Annefrank.

15 Every day about 100 tons (89 t) of material from asteroids fall to Earth. The biggest pieces light up and streak across the sky to create meteors, also known as shooting stars.

1 Jupiter is the **fifth planet from the sun.** It orbits at an average distance of 484 million miles (779 million km), about five times as far from the sun as Earth.

2 JUPITER IS **the largest planet in our solar system. IT WEIGHS MORE THAN ALL THE OTHER PLANETS COMBINED.**

3 JUPITER IS MORE THAN 88,000 MILES (ALMOST 142,000 KM) WIDE AT ITS EQUATOR. IT IS SO LARGE THAT 1,321 Earths could fit inside it.

25 GIANT FACTS ABOUT

4 **Jupiter is not solid** like Earth and the other inner planets. Almost all of the giant planet is made of **hydrogen gas** mixed with a little **helium.** The surface you see in pictures is the upper layer of these gases.

5 It takes Jupiter about 12 years to orbit the sun, meaning if you are 12 years old on Earth, you would have just celebrated your **first** Jupiter birthday.

6 FOR A GIGANTIC PLANET, JUPITER ROTATES INCREDIBLY QUICKLY. ITS DAY— THE TIME IT TAKES JUPITER TO SPIN AROUND ONCE— GOES BY IN JUST **10 HOURS.**

7 **Two dark, thick bands** encircle the planet. Along the broadest band in the Southern Hemisphere is Jupiter's most notable mark: **THE GREAT RED SPOT.**

8 The Great Red Spot is an **enormous storm the size of two Earths.** This churning cyclone rotates counterclockwise at more than **200 miles an hour (322 km/h).**

9 In the last 20 years, **the Great Red Spot has shrunk.** If this trend continues, **the storm could DISAPPEAR** altogether.

10 The **sun** and **Jupiter** are both made mostly of hydrogen and helium, but Jupiter would need to be **70 times more massive** to become even a small star.

11 **You can easily see Jupiter with the naked eye.** Only the moon, Venus, and Mars (on rare occasions) can be brighter in the night sky.

12 Through a telescope, Jupiter looks like **a little disk with stripes.** You can also see four of Jupiter's **many moons** near the planet.

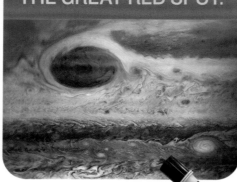

13 Astronomers have discovered at least **79 moons** circling Jupiter. Sixty-three of them are **tiny—**smaller than 6.2 miles (10 km) wide.

14 Italian astronomer **Galileo Galilei** first charted Jupiter's four largest moons and their orbits in 1610. These Galilean moons are named **Io, Europa, Ganymede,** and **Callisto.**

15 Jupiter's moon **Io is the most volcanic place in the solar system.** On Io, volcanoes erupt daily, and some can shoot plumes of lava **250 miles** (402 km) above its surface.

16 A **volcanic crater of molten magma** on Io, named **Loki,** gives off more heat than all the volcanoes on Earth **combined.**

17 JUPITER'S MOON **EUROPA HAS A FROZEN SURFACE.** IT IS BROKEN BY LONG CRACKS AND SHATTERED BY METEOR IMPACTS FROM LONG AGO.

18 Although Europa looks like a **giant ice ball,** it is not frozen solid. Under the ice lies a **vast ocean of liquid water.** Scientists want to explore Europa and search its ocean for **alien life.**

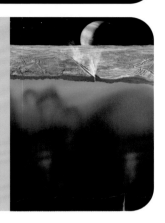

JUPITER

19 **Ganymede** is Jupiter's largest moon and **the biggest moon in the solar system.** At about 3,273 miles (5,267 km) wide, this moon is **larger than the planet Mercury.**

20 Jupiter's moon **Callisto** is nearly the same size as Mercury. It has the **most cratered surface** of any planet or moon in our solar system.

21 In addition to Jupiter's 79 moons, **thousands of rocks** share the planet's orbit. These asteroids, called **Trojans,** circle the sun with Jupiter.

22 Jupiter has **four faint rings.** They are called the halo ring, the main ring, the Amalthea gossamer ring, and the Thebe gossamer ring.

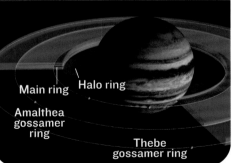

Main ring   Halo ring
Amalthea gossamer ring
Thebe gossamer ring

Nine spacecraft have gotten **close-up views** of Jupiter since 1973: Pioneer 10 and 11, Voyager 1 and 2, Ulysses (on a trip to the sun), Cassini (on its way to Saturn), New Horizons (going to Pluto), Galileo, and Juno (which circled the planet).

23

24 Like Earth, Jupiter has **northern and southern lights called auroras.** They are **created by Jupiter's magnetic field,** the strongest such field of any planet.

25 The **gravity on Jupiter is intense.** If you weighed **100 pounds** (45 kg) on Earth, you would weigh about **240 pounds** (109 kg) on Jupiter (if you could stand on the planet).

1 Saturn is the **sixth planet from the sun,** orbiting at an average distance of 886 million miles (1.4 billion km).

2 At 75,000 miles (120,700 km) in diameter, Saturn is the **second largest planet** in the solar system.

3 Saturn **spins once every 10.5 hours** (a Saturn day), but **it takes 29.4 years to orbit the sun** (a Saturn year).

4 Saturn spins so fast that it bulges at its equator and squishes at the poles. This makes it **the flattest**—or least round—planet in the solar system.

5 Saturn is **less dense than water.** That means that if you built a bathtub large enough to hold Saturn and filled it with water, **Saturn would float.**

25 RINGING FACTS ABOUT

6 If you weigh 100 pounds (45 kg) on Earth, **you would weigh 107 pounds (49 kg) on Saturn.**

7 Saturn is known as the ringed planet because it has **the biggest ring system of any world** in our solar system. The main rings stretch out for **175,000 miles** (almost 282,000 km).

8 SATURN'S RINGS ARE MADE OF **millions of bits of ice and dust that reflect the light of the sun.** THEY MAY HAVE COME FROM MANY MOONS THAT COLLIDED OR WERE RIPPED UP BY SATURN'S INTENSE GRAVITY.

9 EACH OF SATURN'S RINGS ORBITS THE PLANET AT A DIFFERENT RATE. **THE INNER RINGS ORBIT FASTER THAN THE OUTER RINGS.**

10 On average, Saturn's rings are only **100 feet (30 m) thick.** But in some parts of the rings, **ice and dust** have clumped together into larger **boulders and mountains.**

11 Saturn is **tilted** on its axis by 27 degrees. This gives it **seasons** similar to those on Earth—but each season lasts almost **30 times as long.**

12 WHEN SATURN'S RINGS APPEAR **tipped up or down** IN OUR TELESCOPES, **it is summer and winter** ON SATURN. WHEN THEY LOOK **flat,** THAT MARKS **spring and fall.**

13 When the astronomer **Galileo first spied Saturn** and its rings in his telescope in 1610, he didn't know what he was seeing. He explained his blurry view as best he could when he wrote, **"Saturn has ears."**

14 When the rings are pointing directly at Earth, they are **so thin** that they are invisible through even **the most powerful telescopes.**

15 SATURN HAS AT LEAST **82 KNOWN MOONS,** INCLUDING SEVERAL THAT ORBIT WITHIN THE RINGS.

16 Astronomers believe that **tiny moons** orbiting near Saturn **help the planet keep its rings.** Gravity from the tiny moons stops the ring bits from falling into the planet or shooting off into space.

17 The tiny, five-mile (8-km)-wide moon **Daphnis** is nicknamed the **"wave maker"** because it leaves **a visible wave** in whatever ring bits it flies by.

18 **Titan** is Saturn's **largest moon.** At about 3,200 miles (5,150 km) wide, Titan is **a little bigger than the planet Mercury.**

SATURN

19 Titan has **lakes and seas of liquid methane** (a colorless gas) on its surface. Islands of rock and ice rise above the waves of these seas.

20 A ROBOTIC SPACECRAFT NAMED **HUYGENS** LANDED ON TITAN IN 2005 AND IS STILL THERE.

25 You can see Saturn with the naked eye. It looks like a bright yellow star. Saturn is at its biggest and brightest in the nighttime sky every 54 weeks, when it is closest to Earth.

21 Saturn's moon **Mimas** is often nicknamed the **"Death Star moon."** It has a giant crater that makes it look like the moon-size space station from the *Star Wars* movies.

22 Geysers shoot into space on **Enceladus,** a small ice-covered moon of Saturn. As Enceladus orbits Saturn, it leaves behind its own **ring of icy material.**

23 A **raging hurricane** with a hexagonal (six-sided) shape swirls on the north pole of Saturn. The 20,000-mile (32,187-km)-wide storm is **fed by jets of gas** circling below the surface.

24 Saturn has had **four earthly visitors.** Three spacecraft flew by the ringed planet (**Pioneer 11** in 1979, **Voyager 1** in 1980, and **Voyager 2** in 1981), and **the Cassini** orbiter circled it from 2004 to 2017.

1 Uranus was the first planet discovered using **a telescope.** English astronomer William Herschel spotted it **in 1781.**

2 Herschel wanted to name his planet after the King of England, George III. Other astronomers wanted to name it "Herschel." Eventually a more traditional name from ancient mythology—Uranus—was selected.

3 In ancient mythology, Uranus was the **Greek god of the sky.** He was known as the father of Saturn (who was the father of Jupiter), which made him a logical choice for this planet.

4 A day on Uranus is only **17 hours long,** but it takes Uranus **84 years** to complete one orbit around the sun.

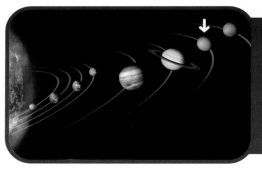

5 Uranus is the **seventh planet from the sun.** It orbits about 1.8 billion miles (2.9 billion km) from the center of the solar system.

6 Uranus is tipped on its side, so it sometimes looks like a green-blue ball rolling around the sun.

7 Uranus is **much larger than Earth.** It has four times the width, takes up 63 times more space, and weighs more than **14 times the mass** of our planet.

Uranus viewed from one of its moons

ABOUT URANUS

8 Uranus is a gas giant like Jupiter and Saturn—you cannot stand on its surface. It is made almost entirely of hydrogen and helium gases.

9 Uranus has the second largest and second brightest rings in the solar system. Its 13 rings are much more dramatic than Jupiter's or Neptune's, but still dim compared to Saturn's.

10 Astronomers recorded the coldest temperature of any planet in Uranus's cloud tops. The temperature in the atmosphere in one area was minus 371°F (-224°C).

11 It is extremely rare, but people with exceptional eyesight can see Uranus with their naked eye. Everyone else needs a pair of binoculars or a telescope to spot it.

12 Unlike the other gas giant planets, Uranus appears to have few surface features. It does have storms and changing weather patterns, but the top gas layer almost always looks like a hazy blue-green ball.

13 Uranus has 27 known moons. The moons Titania and Oberon are the biggest and brightest, but even they look like tiny dots through a large telescope.

14 Some of Uranus's moons—such as Miranda, Ophelia, and Juliet—are named for characters from Shakespeare's plays. Others, like Umbriel, Ariel, and Belinda, come from a poem by Alexander Pope, a 17th-century English writer.

15 Uranus's moon Miranda has mountains of ice. This one, named Verona Rupes, has a cliff six miles (9.6 km) high—taller than Earth's Mount Everest. If you jumped off that cliff, it would take you eight minutes to land on the ground.

15 STORMY FACTS

❶ Neptune is the **eighth and farthest** planet from the sun. On average, it orbits **2.8 billion miles** (4.5 billion km) out.

❷ Traveling at an average of about 12,158 miles an hour (19,556 km/h), Neptune is the **slowest-moving planet.** At that speed, it takes about **165 years to orbit the sun.**

❸ Neptune's day is about **16 hours long.** That is shorter than Earth's day, but **longer than that of Jupiter or Saturn.**

❹ Neptune appears to have **a deep watery blue color** through a telescope. That is why astronomers who first saw it thought it should be named after **the Roman god of the sea.**

❺ It may look watery, but the surface of Neptune is blue because of **a little extra methane gas in its atmosphere.** Swimming there would be deadly!

❻ Like the other gassy planets, Neptune doesn't have a solid surface. It's made of **a combination of hydrogen, helium, and other gases.**

❼ Neptune is **the windiest planet.** Astronomers have clocked steady winds of 1,300 miles an hour (2,092 km/h) in its blue and white cloud tops. That's 10 times **stronger than a strong hurricane** on Earth.

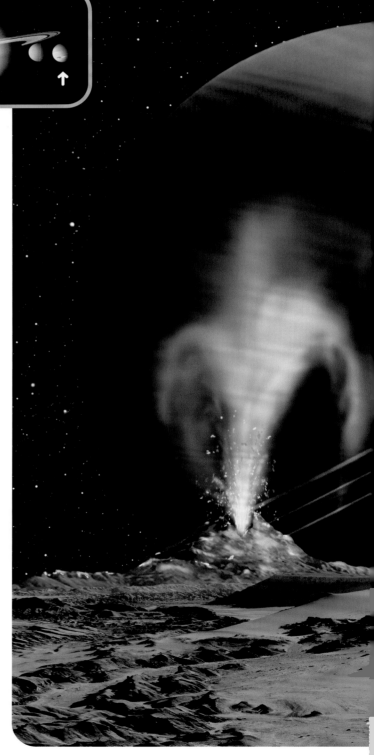

ABOUT NEPTUNE

Neptune seen from its moon Triton

8 Astronomers can see **a lot of weather happening** on Neptune. High, light-colored clouds often circle the planet. Dark storms, including a huge one called **the Great Dark Spot**, stir up the atmosphere.

9 Neptune and Earth are the fourth and fifth largest planets in our solar system. Neptune is almost **four times as wide** and **weighs 17 times more** than Earth.

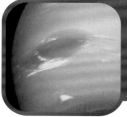

10 Neptune has **14 known moons.** In keeping with Neptune's nautical theme, these moons are named after **minor water gods from Greek mythology,** including Triton, Naiad, and Nereid.

11 Triton, Neptune's largest moon, is one of **the coldest places** in the solar system. Temperatures there are about minus 391°F (-235°C).

12 Neptune's **five rings** are extremely dark and can barely be seen. Astronomers found them when their **shadowy outlines** came in front of and blocked out the light of more distant stars.

13 John Couch Adams and Urbain Le Verrier **predicted the existence of Neptune using math.** Before actually seeing it, Le Verrier told astronomers to point their telescopes to a certain spot. When they did, **they found Neptune.**

14 Only the Voyager 2 spacecraft has **flown close to either Uranus or Neptune.** It left Earth in 1977, and zoomed past Neptune in 1989.

15 Because Neptune is so far away, it is **not visible to the naked eye.** In fact, you need a powerful backyard telescope just to see it as **a tiny dot.**

1

Although there may be many more, **five objects** in space have been officially named dwarf planets: Pluto, Eris, Makemake, Haumea, and Ceres.

2

To be a dwarf planet, an object must **go around the sun**. It must also be large enough and have enough gravity to form into a **nearly spherical** (round) shape.

3

Unlike regular planets, dwarf planets are not the bosses of their part of the solar system. They **share their orbits** with a lot of similar objects.

4

American astronomer Clyde Tombaugh discovered **Pluto** in 1930. Eleven-year-old **Venetia Burney** suggested the name Pluto, and it has stuck ever since.

5

Pluto was considered **a planet until 2006**, when astronomers voted to place it in a new category: **dwarf planet.**

6

It takes Pluto **248 years** to travel once around the sun—a journey of 3.7 billion miles (5.9 billion km), on average.

7

Pluto has a **stretched-out orbit** that takes it from about 4.6 billion miles (7.4 billion km) to as close as 2.8 billion miles (4.5 billion km) away from the sun.

8

Between 1979 and 1999, Pluto was **closer to the sun** than Neptune was. That won't happen again until 2227.

9

Although on maps of the solar system Neptune's and Pluto's orbits look like they cross, **the planets will never run into each other.** In three-dimensional space, their orbits don't overlap and never cross paths.

10

Pluto is a spherical **ball of ice and rock** 1,474 miles (2,372 km) in diameter. That's about the distance a plane flies from Washington, D.C., to Denver, Colorado, U.S.A.

11

To different people, the **big light-colored area** on Pluto's surface looks like a heart, or a whale's tail, or even the face of the Disney character Pluto.

12

Although Pluto is mostly covered in ice, it may have an **ocean of water** just below the frozen surface.

13

Pluto has **slow-moving glaciers** made of nitrogen ice. They carve huge grooves on the surface.

14

Even though Pluto is so small, it is big enough to hold on to an atmosphere. In fact, the color of **the sky on Pluto would be blue.**

15

Pluto has **five moons:** Charon, Nix, Hydra, Styx, and Kerberos. Charon, Pluto's largest moon, is about **half the size of Pluto.**

16

Charon is so massive that it does not simply orbit Pluto. Pluto and Charon orbit each other and are often thought to be a **double planet.**

17

Pluto and Charon **face each other all the time.** Pluto rotates once every 6.4 days, and Charon revolves around Pluto once **every 6.4 days.**

18

Pluto has had **only one robotic visitor** from Earth. The New Horizons spacecraft flew through space for 9.5 years before flying by Pluto in 2015.

19

Eris is another round dwarf planet in the far reaches of the solar system. It was discovered in 2005, orbiting more than **6 billion miles** (9.7 billion km) from the sun.

20

Eris's discoverers originally nicknamed it **Xena,** after the main character in the TV series *Xena: Warrior Princess.* But the dwarf planet was soon given its official name of Eris, the **goddess of conflict** in Greek mythology.

21

Eris has one moon, named **Dysnomia,** that circles the dwarf planet every 16 days. In Greek mythology, Dysnomia was **Eris's daughter,** known for lawlessness.

22

When **Eris** was first discovered, some astronomers considered it to be the **10th planet,** because it was about the same size as Pluto (which was then still considered a planet). However, astronomers now consider it a dwarf planet.

23

Until 2015, astronomers believed that **Eris** might even be larger than Pluto. Then **New Horizons** measured Pluto accurately. At 1,445 miles (2,326 km) in diameter, Eris is smaller.

24

Eris's surface is **covered in white ice** and is **more reflective** than any other planet or dwarf planet. Only Saturn's moon Enceladus is shinier.

25

Another dwarf planet, **Haumea,** is a strange, **football-shaped** object that rotates every four hours.

26

Haumea is about 1,440 miles (2,317 km) across at its widest point, but only **619 miles (996 km) wide** at its skinniest spot.

27

At an average distance of about 4 billion miles (6.4 billion km), it takes Haumea about **285 years** to circle the sun.

28

Haumea has two small moons, **Hi'iaka and Namaka.** Namaka goes around Haumea every 18 days, while Hi'iaka takes 49 days.

29
Haumea has faint rings. It is the farthest object from the sun known to have these accessories.

30
Scientists think that Haumea **collided with another object** a long time ago, and that's what created its football shape, two moons, and rings.

31
Makemake, another dwarf planet, takes about **305 years** to make one complete orbit.

32
Smaller than Pluto and Eris, but more massive than Haumea, Makemake is only about **888 miles (1,430 km)** wide.

33
In 2016, astronomers announced they found **one moon around Makemake.** It does not have an official name yet.

34
The surface of Makemake is so cold (about minus 469°F [-278°C]) that **it is coated in ice** made of methane, ethane, and nitrogen.

35
Along with thousands of other objects, Makemake formed in a region of space beyond Neptune called **the Kuiper belt.**

36
Italian astronomer **Giuseppe Piazzi** discovered Ceres on January 1, 1801. He named it after the **ancient Roman harvest goddess.**

37
Unlike all the other asteroids in the asteroid belt, **Ceres** is large enough to have **a nearly round shape.** This is why astronomers call it a dwarf planet.

38
Earth is about 2,400 times larger than Ceres. In fact, Ceres is **much smaller than Earth's moon.**

39
Ceres used to only be known as the solar system's largest asteroid. Now, at just 592 miles (952 km) in diameter, it's also considered to be the **smallest dwarf planet.**

40
In 2015, NASA sent the **Dawn spacecraft** to circle and explore Ceres up close. It was the **first mission to visit a dwarf planet.**

41
The Dawn mission took close-up pictures of **two bright white spots** on Ceres. They may be places where **salt formed** after water boiled away.

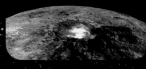

42
It takes Ceres **nine hours to spin one time** (its day), and 4.6 years to orbit the sun one time (its year).

43
Ceres doesn't have many craters. Astronomers think that water ice and salts on the surface have smoothed away the old craters.

44
Between the orbits of Jupiter and Neptune float a number of small objects, similar to both asteroids and comets, called **Centaurs.** Scientists don't know a lot about them yet.

45
Several objects in the outer solar system are almost big enough to be dwarf planets. These include **Sedna, Quaoar, Orcus,** and **Gonggong.**

46
Quaoar is 800 miles (1,287 km) in diameter **with one tiny moon.** It circles the sun at an average distance of 4 billion miles (6.4 billion km).

47
Astronomers discovered **Sedna** in 2003. About 1,100 miles (1,770 km) in diameter, it is about three-quarters the size of Pluto.

48
Sedna is about **three times farther** from the sun than Pluto. It takes about 10,500 years to go around the sun one time.

49
Sedna has an extremely **oval-shaped orbit.** At its closest, Sedna is still more than 7 billion miles (11 billion km) from the sun. But when farthest from the sun, it is more than **100 billion miles** (161 billion km) away.

50
'Oumuamua is a long, skinny, rocky, **cometlike object** that passed near Earth in 2017. It was the **first object** we've seen visiting us from another solar system.

50 MASSIVE FACTS ABOUT DWARF PLANETS and Other Small Worlds

Dwarf planet Pluto

1 Comets are **frozen chunks of ice, dust, and rock** that circle the sun in oval paths. They are often nicknamed **"dirty snowballs."**

2 AS A COMET COMES CLOSER TO THE SUN, **it heats up.** GASES FLY OFF ITS SURFACE TO CREATE **A TAIL.**

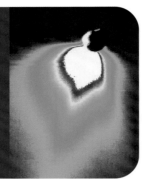

3 Comets have **four main parts:** the **nucleus, coma, dust tail,** and **ion tail.**

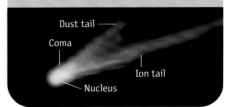

Dust tail
Coma
Ion tail
Nucleus

4 The **nucleus** is the **only solid part** of a comet. It is usually between a few miles and **tens of miles wide.**

5 The **coma** is a comet's atmosphere: a see-through envelope of **gas surrounding the nucleus.**

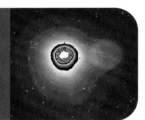

25 SNOWY FACTS ABOUT

6 The coma can be **larger than a planet.**

7

The **ion tail** is made of **gases blown off the comet by solar wind**—a constant stream of particles flying away from the sun.

8 A comet's **dust tail** is made of bits of ice and dust that **erupted off the comet** after the sun heated its surface.

9 COMETS THAT TAKE LESS THAN 200 YEARS TO GO AROUND THE SUN ARE CALLED **short-period comets.** COMETS THAT TAKE MORE THAN 200 YEARS ARE **long-period comets.**

10 **Short-period comets** come from a region of the solar system called **the Kuiper belt.** This is about 30 to 100 times farther from the sun than Earth is.

11 **Long-period comets** come from the **Oort cloud,** a vast region of space 2,000 to 100,000 times farther away from the sun than Earth is.

12 Astronomers have observed **MORE THAN 3,600 COMETS** orbiting the sun.

13 If you discover a comet, you can officially **name it after yourself.**

14 In the distant past, **comets were a source of fear.** They appeared without warning, casting their long tails across the sky.

15

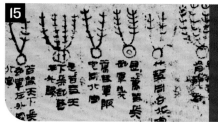

Ancient Chinese astronomers were the best comet-watchers in the world. They kept track of the appearances and movements of comets and even **drew extensive pictures** of what they looked like.

17 Comet **HALE-BOPP,** which came near Earth in 1997, had the **largest nucleus** ever observed, at 60 miles (97 km) wide.

18 Stretching more than 360 million miles (579 million km), **comet Hyakutake's tail was the longest** astronomers have ever seen.

16 Some astronomers believe that comets **may have brought water** and other compounds important for life to Earth when our planet was young.

19 THE MOST FAMOUS COMET IS **HALLEY'S COMET.** IT COMES NEAR EARTH **EVERY 76 YEARS** ON ITS WAY AROUND THE SUN.

COMETS

20 French astronomer **Charles Messier** was known as the "comet ferret." He discovered more than a dozen comets in the 1700s and 1800s.

21 NASA's **SOHO space observatory** has found nearly **3,000 comets** while studying the region **around the sun.**

22 The **Great Comet of 1744** was one of the **brightest** ever seen. For a little while, it even showed **six tails.**

23 Canadian astronomer **David Levy** discovered 22 comets by himself or with his **friends Gene and Carolyn Shoemaker.** They included comet **Shoemaker-Levy 9,** which smashed into Jupiter in 1994.

25

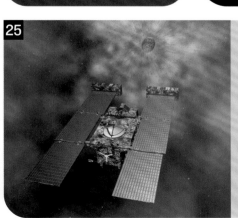

NASA'S STARDUST MISSION FLEW THROUGH THE TAIL OF **COMET WILD 2.** THEN IT BROUGHT PIECES OF THE COMET BACK TO EARTH.

24 The **brightest comet** of the 20th century was comet **Ikeya-Seki.** In 1965, it shined brighter than a full moon.

1 The word "astronaut" comes from the Greek words for "star sailor." Russian astronauts are called cosmonauts— "universe sailors."

2 **NASA** stands for the National Aeronautics and Space Administration. Formed in 1958, this agency is in charge of American piloted and robotic space missions. It also carries out scientific research into spaceflight and astronomy.

3 Russia's space agency is called **Roscosmos**. It regularly launches rockets into space, which carry satellites into orbit and crews of cosmonauts to the **International Space Station (ISS).**

4 The European Space Agency **(ESA)** trains astronauts from various countries in Europe. It has led many important **robotic missions** in space.

5 Many other countries, including **China, India, Canada, Japan, Australia, Israel,** and **South Africa,** also have space programs.

25 ROCKETING FACTS ABOUT

7 IF YOU BLASTED OFF FROM EARTH IN A ROCKET DESIGNED FOR HUMAN MISSIONS, YOU'D REACH SPACE IN ABOUT TWO MINUTES, 30 SECONDS.

6 Although it's tough to say exactly **where Earth's atmosphere ends** and outer space begins, American scientists consider anything beyond **62 miles** (100 km) from Earth as **"space."**

8 **To orbit Earth,** a spacecraft must reach a speed of at least 17,500 miles an hour (28,164 km/h). It normally takes about **eight and a half minutes** to get to this speed.

9 **Vostok I,** the first rocket to launch a human into space, stood about **125 feet (38 m) tall.** It weighed over 287 tons (256 t).

10 **The force** astronauts feel during launch is **measured in "g."** One g is the normal force you feel in Earth's gravity.

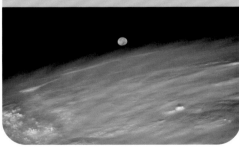

11 Astronauts typically experience **THREE G** during takeoff. This makes their bodies feel **three times heavier** than normal.

12 During launch, astronauts **lie back in their chairs** to absorb the tremendous forces caused by their rocket's increasing speed.

13

When orbiting Earth, you feel **weightless.** But in fact you are in **microgravity,** where g-forces are almost, but not quite, **zero.**

14 Astronauts circling Earth are **still being pulled down by the planet's gravity.** However, they are traveling so fast that they never hit the ground. Essentially, they keep falling and missing Earth.

15

NASA's **space shuttles** were the first **REUSABLE SPACE VEHICLES.** They were big enough to have a crew of seven people while also delivering large satellites into orbit.

16 **Five space shuttles** (named *Columbia, Challenger, Discovery, Endeavour,* and *Atlantis*) flew more than 513 million miles (826 million km) combined over **30 years of missions.**

17 The **ISS** orbits about 250 miles (402 km) above Earth, which is roughly the length of **4,400 football fields.**

18 AFTER THE MOON AND THE PLANET VENUS, **THE ISS IS THE THIRD BRIGHTEST OBJECT** VISIBLE TO THE NAKED EYE IN THE NIGHTTIME SKY.

SPACE TRAVEL

19 **To become an astronaut,** you must go through **years of training.** You practice takeoffs, landings, and living in low gravity all on Earth.

20 To practice in weightless conditions, astronauts **train underwater** in NASA's Neutral Buoyancy Lab, a pool so large it **can hold a whole spacecraft.**

21 American astronauts traditionally must be between **five feet two and a half inches to six feet three inches** (159 to 191 cm) tall to fly in a NASA mission. But there were exceptions. At six feet four inches (193 cm), Jim Wetherbee was the tallest person to fly in space. Nancy Currie-Gregg was the shortest, at five feet (152 cm) tall.

22 For long space missions, **shorter astronauts** might have an advantage. They take up less space, need less food, and expel less waste. The first person in space, **Soviet cosmonaut Yuri Gagarin,** stood five feet two inches (157 cm) tall.

25 It took **42 separate flights** to send all the parts of the ISS into space, where astronauts put the pieces together, **one by one,** to create a place to live in space.

23 AS OF 2022, MORE THAN 250 DIFFERENT PEOPLE, REPRESENTING **19 DIFFERENT COUNTRIES,** HAVE SPENT TIME IN THE **ISS.**

24 People have been **living in the ISS** since October 31, 2000—**longer than in any other spacecraft.**

1 The National Aeronautics and Space Administration (NASA) created **the Apollo program** in 1961 to take humans to the moon and return them safely to Earth.

2 Between 1969 and 1972, **six Apollo missions** landed crews on the moon's surface: Apollo 11, 12, 14, 15, 16, and 17.

3 Apollo crews had **three astronauts each.** When they reached the moon, **two** astronauts went to the surface in a lunar module while **one** stayed in the capsule circling above.

4 **Twenty-four** astronauts have flown around the moon. **Twelve** of them walked on the lunar surface.

5 THREE ASTRONAUTS TRAVELED TO THE MOON **TWICE:** JIM LOVELL, JOHN YOUNG, AND GENE CERNAN. YOUNG AND CERNAN **WALKED ON THE MOON'S SURFACE** ON THEIR SECOND TRIP.

25 ADVENTUROUS
FACTS ABOUT THE

6 The **Saturn V rocket** propelled every U.S. spacecraft that went to the moon. It was as tall as a 36-story building, weighed 6.5 million pounds (2.9 million kg), and remains the **largest launch vehicle** ever used.

7 In 1968, Frank Borman, Jim Lovell, and William Anders on **Apollo 8** were the **first people to orbit the moon.** They were the first humans to see the far side of the moon with their own eyes.

8 **APOLLO II** landed the **first people on the moon.** It was crewed by Neil Armstrong, Buzz Aldrin, and Michael Collins, and launched from Kennedy Space Center, Florida, U.S.A., on July 16, 1969.

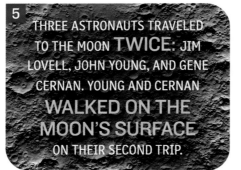

9 While Neil Armstrong and Buzz Aldrin headed down to the moon's surface, astronaut **Michael Collins** watched them from above. He wasn't lonely. He called the capsule circling the moon his **"happy little home."**

10 At the last minute, Armstrong had to carefully guide the lunar module (nicknamed *Eagle*) to a new landing spot to avoid **crashing into boulders.**

11

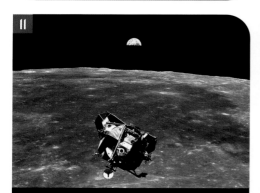

The lunar module was **almost out of fuel.** If Armstrong had taken 30 seconds more in flying around, the astronauts would have been sent home without touching the moon.

12 **Buzz Aldrin** uttered the first words ever spoken on the moon's surface. Upon touchdown he said, **"OKAY, ENGINES STOP,"** a moment before Neil Armstrong said, **"THE EAGLE HAS LANDED."**

13 Armstrong suited up, opened the door, climbed down the ladder, and became the first person to set foot on the moon. He declared, **"That's one small step for [a] man, one giant leap for mankind."**

42

14 Altogether, Armstrong and Aldrin spent only **21 hours and 38 minutes** on the moon.

15  Armstrong and Aldrin collected 48 pounds (22 kg) of **moon rocks** during their brief stay on the surface and brought them home to Earth for study.

16 Because the gravity on the moon is one-sixth that of Earth, the astronauts developed their own ways of **walking, skipping, or hopping** on the surface. **They still fell down a lot.**

17 The Apollo 11 astronauts traveled more than **1,096,348 miles** (1,764,401 km) during their eight-day journey to the moon and back. That's like flying **more than 440 times between New York and Los Angeles.**

18 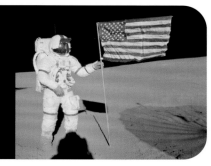 Each U.S. moon mission planted **an American flag** on the surface. The flags had metal rods in them so they would stand up in the airless environment.

FIRST HUMANS ON THE MOON

19 To prepare for the **lower gravity** on the moon, Armstrong and Aldrin trained on Earth by **walking sideways on a wall** while held up by wires.

20 When Armstrong, Aldrin, and Collins returned to Earth, they were placed **in quarantine for 21 days** in case they brought back any **moon germs.**

21 Astronaut Alan Shepard smuggled a **golf club and golf balls** to the moon on Apollo 14. He joked that a ball he hit there went "miles and miles!" (According to a photo, more like 650 feet [200 m].)

22 Apollo 15, 16, and 17 brought a lunar roving vehicle— a **"moon buggy"**— for the astronauts to drive. It let them explore farther than previous missions.

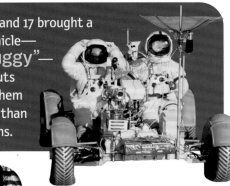

23 Astronauts returning to the lunar module tracked in **moon dust** on their boots. Some of them thought it smelled like gunpowder or wet ashes from a fireplace.

24  The last person to leave boot prints on the moon was astronaut **Gene Cernan.** No human has been back since that day: **December 14, 1972.**

25 Decades after the final Apollo mission, a robotic spacecraft orbiting the moon captured images of the six landing sites. **The paths the astronauts trod** on the dusty soil of the moon could still be seen.

1 In 1960, space mission SPUTNIK 5 rocketed TWO DOGS—Belka and Strelka—40 MICE, two rats, and some plants around Earth.

2 In 1966, the first astronauts, two Soviet dogs named VETEROK AND UGOLYOK, remained in space for 22 DAYS.

3 In 1968, Soviet spacecraft Zond 5 carried TURTLES, FLIES, MEALWORMS, AND BACTERIA on a seven-day trip around the moon.

4 On April 12, 1961, Soviet cosmonaut YURI GAGARIN became the first person to reach space and orbit Earth.

5 Just before liftoff, Gagarin exclaimed, "POYEKHALI!," which means "LET'S GO!"

11 When astronauts put on a SPACE SUIT and leave their craft, it's officially called an extravehicular activity, or SPACE WALK.

12 Soviet cosmonaut ALEKSEI LEONOV performed the first space walk in 1965 when he floated outside his craft for 12 minutes.

18 With almost no gravity to weigh him down on the ISS, SCOTT KELLY returned to Earth TWO INCHES (5 CM) TALLER.

19 ASTRONAUTS living on the International Space Station have completed more than 200 SPACE WALKS.

25 In 2004, Michael Melvill piloted SpaceShipOne, the first spacecraft BUILT BY A PRIVATE COMPANY.

26 At 25 years old, Gherman Titov was the youngest person to go into space. He also was the FIRST TO SLEEP IN SPACE.

Astronaut Bruce McCandless in an untethered space walk

35 HIGH-FLYING FACTS ABOUT

6 When Gagarin's mission was over, he landed in a field MORE THAN 100 MILES (161 KM) OFF TARGET.

7 The FIRST WOMAN to go into space was cosmonaut Valentina Tereshkova. She flew on the Soviet craft Vostok 6 in 1963.

8 Alan Shepard was the FIRST AMERICAN to reach space. His trip lasted only 15 MINUTES AND 22 SECONDS.

9 In 1962, JOHN GLENN became the first American to orbit Earth. When he became weightless, he said, "Zero g, and I feel fine."

10 When John Glenn flew again aboard the space shuttle *Discovery* in 1998, at the age of 77, he became the OLDEST PERSON to orbit Earth.

13 When they returned to Earth, the cosmonauts from Voskhod 2 LANDED OFF TARGET in an uninhabited forest.

14 The Voskhod 2 cosmonauts had to spend one night in their capsule and another IN A HUT before being rescued.

15 Russian Valery Polyakov spent 438 days aboard the Mir space station, the LONGEST STAY by any person on a single flight.

16 Russian cosmonaut Gennady Padalka has spent MORE TIME IN SPACE than any other human: 878 DAYS.

17 From 2015 to 2016, American Scott Kelly spent almost ONE YEAR IN SPACE. His twin brother, Mark, is also an astronaut.

20 In 1959, 13 WOMEN completed extensive astronaut training, but were not allowed into the astronaut program.

21 The first American woman in space was SALLY RIDE, who flew aboard the space shuttle *Challenger* in 1983.

22 In 1998, aboard the space shuttle *Endeavour*, DR. MAE JEMISON was the FIRST African American woman in space.

23 American astronaut CHRISTINA KOCH spent 328 days in space on the ISS—the longest space mission by any woman.

24 Dennis Tito was the first "SPACE TOURIST." In 2001, he paid the Russian government $20 MILLION for a ride.

27 The crew of Apollo 13 has been FARTHER FROM EARTH than any other humans.

28 When the Apollo 13 astronauts circled the far side of the moon in 1970, they were 248,655 MILES (400,171 km) from Earth.

29 The FASTEST SPEED any human has traveled in space (or anywhere) was 24,791 miles an hour (39,897 km/h).

30 The crew of APOLLO 10 reached this speed on their way back to Earth after circling the moon.

31 American astronauts Franklin Chang-Diaz and Jerry Ross have each gone into space SEVEN DIFFERENT TIMES.

32 In 1984, Bruce McCandless took the FIRST UNTETHERED SPACE WALK (not connected to the ship by a cord).

33 Anatoly Solovyev took a record 16 SPACE WALKS and spent 82 hours outside his spacecraft.

34 GUY BLUFORD was the FIRST African American man to go into space, aboard the space shuttle *Challenger* in 1983.

35 Susan Helms and James Voss accomplished the LONGEST SPACE WALK—eight hours and 56 minutes.

ASTRONAUT ACHIEVEMENTS

1

The Soviet Union launched the first artificial satellite, Sputnik, into orbit on October 4, 1957. It was the size of a large beach ball.

2

NASA's Explorer 6 satellite, which circled Earth in 1959, sent back the first pictures of our planet taken from outer space.

3

In 1962, NASA's Mariner 2 spacecraft completed the first flyby of another planet when it zoomed just above Venus's surface.

4

The Soviet Union launched Luna 1 in 1959, with the goal of crashing into the moon. It quickly went off course. Today, the dead spacecraft is circling the sun.

5

Luna 2 made it to the moon and smacked into the lunar surface on September 14, 1959. It was the first craft to land on anything in space.

6

The first spacecraft to fly by Mercury was NASA's Mariner 10. On the way, it flew past Venus and then looped around Mercury three times between 1974 and 1975.

7

It took Mariner 4 eight months to reach Mars in 1965. From a distance of 6,118 miles (9,846 km), it sent back the first close-up images of the Martian surface.

8

NASA's twin robotic landers, Viking 1 and Viking 2, took the first color panoramic pictures of the Martian landscape.

9

Sojourner was the first Mars rover. It rolled around Mars's surface for 83 days. It was driven by radio signals from scientists on Earth, millions of miles away.

10

The Spirit and Opportunity rovers explored Mars beginning in 2004. After landing on opposite sides of the planet, they checked out craters and climbed small mountains.

11

Spirit was active for 6 years and traveled 4.8 miles (7.7 km) on Mars. Opportunity kept rolling on the red planet for 14 years and covered 28 miles (45 km).

12

The newest rover on Mars is called Perseverance. Its mission is to look for signs of life and set aside interesting rock samples that could eventually be sent to Earth.

13

NASA's Phoenix mission landed a probe near the north pole on Mars in hopes of finding water. When its robotic shovel dug into the Martian soil, it hit a patch of ice, confirming that Mars does indeed have water.

14

India's robotic craft Mangalyaan is orbiting Mars and studying the Martian atmosphere. It has a fun nickname: Mars Orbiter Mission, or MOM for short.

15

NASA's Odyssey spacecraft has been circling and studying Mars since 2001. It is one of the longest-lasting missions to study another world.

16

The Soviet Union's Luna 3 was the first spacecraft to fly past the far side of the moon. It sent back pictures of a lunar surface never before seen by human eyes.

17

The Chinese lander Chang'e 4 and its rover Yutu 2 were the first to explore the far side of the moon in an area near the lunar south pole.

18

The first orbiting space station was Salyut 1, launched by the Soviet Union in 1971. It circled Earth for 175 days.

19

Three-person crews lived on board the first American space station, Skylab, for 171 days. Then it orbited, empty, for another five years.

20

The Soviet space station Mir was launched in 1986. Russian astronauts kept it circling our planet until 2001, when it fell back to Earth. Cosmonauts lived in Mir for more than 4,500 days.

21

The International Space Station (ISS) is a joint effort between the United States, Russia, and several other countries. It was built in space, piece by piece, starting in 1998.

22

The ISS weighs more than 900,000 pounds (408,233 kg).

50 NIFTY FACTS ABOUT THE COOLEST SPACE MISSIONS

23
The ISS is the most expensive item ever built. By some estimates, it has cost more than $100 billion to build and maintain.

24
The U.S. Air Force is testing out a secret reusable space plane called the X-37B, or OTV. No one knows exactly what it is doing.

25
Although the U.S. Air Force doesn't talk much about the OTV publicly, people in their backyards track its movement and can tell you where to look for it when it flies over your town.

26
The robotic Soviet lunar rover Lunokhod 2 traveled 24 miles (39 km) across the moon in 1973. This eight-wheeled rover held the off-Earth roving record until 2014.

27
The Lunar Reconnaissance Orbiter (LRO) has captured some of the sharpest images of the lunar surface, including the Apollo landing spots.

28
Venus Express, a robotic mission of the European Space Agency (ESA), circled Venus from 2006 to 2014. It found signs of an ancient ocean and discovered that Venus has more lightning strikes than Earth.

29
When Venus Express ran out of fuel, it crashed into the planet. But before it burned up completely, it sent back important information about the Venusian atmosphere.

30
Pulled by the gravity of the sun, the Parker Solar Probe is the fastest spacecraft ever. It has zoomed through space at 244,225 miles an hour (393,042 km/h) to study the sun up close.

31
The Galileo mission orbited Jupiter from 1995 to 2003 and sent back close-up images and data. Scientists ended the mission by crashing Galileo into Jupiter to stop it from smacking into the moon Europa.

32
Before crashing, Galileo repeatedly flew by Jupiter's four largest moons (Io, Europa, Ganymede, and Callisto) and helped scientists on Earth create maps of these distant moons.

33
NASA's Juno mission got close-up views of the storms swirling around Jupiter's poles and uncovered details about the Great Red Spot.

34
The Cassini spacecraft was the first to orbit Saturn. It spent 13 years studying the planet, its rings, and its moons.

35
Cassini took several pictures of Earth from Saturn. Our planet looks like a tiny dot.

36
Flying so close to Saturn's rings, Cassini captured stunning images of small moons and the waves they create in the rings.

37
The ESA's Huygens lander hitched a ride on the Cassini spacecraft. Huygens then parachuted safely onto Titan, Saturn's largest moon. It was the first landing in the outer solar system.

38
As Cassini's fuel supplies ran low, scientists intentionally crashed it into Saturn to study the gas giant's upper atmosphere.

39
The Soviet Union's Vega 1 spacecraft had two missions: After it left a lander and a balloon on Venus in 1986, it took a close-up look at Halley's comet.

40
On July 4, 2005, NASA intentionally crashed a probe named Deep Impact into the Tempel 1 comet to see what materials were hidden below the comet's surface.

41
Japan's Hayabusa mission landed on asteroid Itokawa, collected pieces from the surface, and then flew them back to Earth. They dropped by parachute into Australia, where scientists collected them for study.

42
The Hayabusa 2 spacecraft circled the asteroid Ryugu and landed rovers on its tiny surface. Like the first Hayabusa, it sent samples back to Earth.

43
In 1972, Pioneer 10 became the first spacecraft to fly through the asteroid belt between Mars and Jupiter on its way to Jupiter. Pioneer 11 followed behind in 1973 and made the first close-up visit to Saturn.

44
The Voyager 1 and Voyager 2 missions blasted off from Earth in the summer of 1977 to visit the outer solar system. They are still communicating with our planet.

45
The Voyager 2 mission completed a "Grand Tour" by flying past all four of the gas giant planets: Jupiter, Saturn, Uranus, and Neptune.

46
Voyager 1 is flying out of the solar system at about 320 million miles (515 million km) a year, while Voyager 2 is zooming away from us at about 290 million miles (467 million km) a year.

47
Each Voyager spacecraft carries a golden record with greetings in many languages, nature sounds of Earth, images, and music. If aliens ever find one, there are even instructions for them on how to play it.

48
At more than 14 billion miles (almost 23 billion km) from Earth, the Voyager 1 spacecraft is the farthest human-made object in space.

49
NASA's New Horizons was the fastest spacecraft launched from Earth, leaving the planet at more than 36,000 miles an hour (57,936 km/h).

50
New Horizons has visited the farthest objects in our solar system.

1 Ancient Greek philosopher **Thales of Miletus** was the first person to accurately predict an **eclipse.** He correctly forecast that the moon would cover the sun on May 28, 585 B.C.

2 In the fourth century B.C., Chinese astronomer **Shi Shen** was the first to observe and document **sunspots** (storms on the surface of the sun that look like little spots).

3 Around 350 B.C., the Greek philosopher **Aristotle** wrote a book that explained why **Earth was round** and not flat.

4 More than 2,000 years ago, the Greek mathematician **Eratosthenes** measured the way sunlight fell at two different spots on Earth. He then **used geometry** to show that Earth was 24,660 miles (39,686 km) around— really close to the true number.

5 More than 1,500 years ago, **Hypatia** was a leading astronomer and mathematician living in Alexandria, Egypt. She **designed scientific instruments** to chart the stars and improved upon scientific teachings of ancient astronomers.

25 FAMOUS
FACTS ABOUT GREAT

6 Ancient astronomer **Claudius Ptolemy** wrote a book in A.D. 150 that is now known as the *Almagest.* It outlined everything known about the heavens and became the **leading astronomy text for 1,400 years.**

7 In the 10th century, Persian astronomer **Abd al-Rahman al-Sufi** was the first to describe the **Andromeda galaxy.** This galaxy has billions of stars in it but looks only like a tiny cloud of light from Earth.

8 Many of the remote islands in the Pacific Ocean were discovered by Polynesian and Micronesian people who **used only stars and constellations** to guide their boats over vast distances.

9 In 1543, Polish astronomer **Nicolaus Copernicus** was the first to explain the **heliocentric** model of the solar system, which shows that planets circle the sun and not Earth.

10 Danish astronomer **Tycho Brahe** was the first to publish scientific observations of a supernova (in 1572) and a comet (in 1577). His discoveries showed that outer space was constantly changing.

11 In the early 1600s, German astronomer **Johannes Kepler** discovered three mathematical rules that still guide astronomy today. **Kepler's laws** accurately plot the paths that planets take around the sun.

12 Italian astronomer **Galileo Galilei** revolutionized the use of the **telescope** to discover craters on the moon, sunspots, moons of Jupiter, and stars never before seen.

13 In 1655, Dutch astronomer **Christiaan Huygens** discovered Titan, Saturn's largest moon. He was also the first to accurately describe the beautiful **rings of Saturn.**

14

Today's space program wouldn't exist without **Isaac Newton**. In 1686, he published **three laws of motion** that describe how everything moves in space, including planets, moons, and even rockets.

15

Between 1751 and 1753, French astronomer **Nicolas-Louis de Lacaille** was the first person to create a **detailed star map of the night sky** visible from the Southern Hemisphere. He noted the positions of nearly 10,000 stars.

16

Nicole-Reine Lepaute was a French astronomer and mathematician. In the 1760s, she was an expert in **the motion of the planets**, charted a solar eclipse, and helped figure out the path Halley's comet takes around the sun.

17

In 1786, German astronomer **Caroline Herschel** became the **first woman to discover a comet.** She found **seven more comets** over the following 10 years.

18

Caroline Herschel was an incredible observer of star clusters, nebulae, and **galaxies beyond our solar system.**

19

More than 200 years ago, **Benjamin Banneker** became the first well-known African American astronomer after he published a series of books called **almanacs.**

ASTRONOMERS

20

American astronomer **Henrietta Swan Leavitt** created a way to measure the distances to faraway galaxies by observing special stars called **Cepheid variables.**

21

German physicist **Albert Einstein** changed astronomy forever when he showed that **space and time are linked**, and accurately described the motions of everything in the universe.

22

American astronomer **Edwin Hubble** discovered that **the universe is EXPANDING.** He studied distant galaxies and found that they are moving away from the Milky Way at tremendous speed.

23

In the 1960s, American astronomers **Arno Penzias** and **Robert Wilson** discovered a faint radiation reaching Earth from all parts of the night sky. This is the leftover heat from **the beginnings of the universe.**

25

IN 1992, ASTRONOMERS **ALEKSANDER WOLSZCZAN** AND **DALE FRAIL** FOUND THE **FIRST EXOPLANET**—A PLANET BEYOND OUR SOLAR SYSTEM— CIRCLING A COLLAPSED STAR CALLED **A PULSAR.**

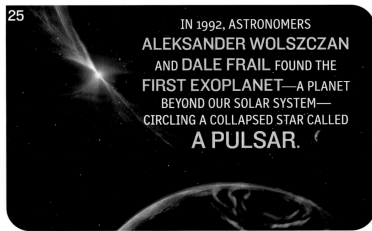

24

American astronomer **Vera Rubin** studied galaxies and found them moving strangely. She was one of the first people to see the effects of **dark matter,** an invisible force that makes up and moves much of our universe.

1 A GALAXY is a humongous collection of stars, gas, and dust that circles around a common center of gravity.

2 Astronomers group galaxies into categories based on their shapes. The three main types are elliptical, irregular, and spiral.

3 Elliptical galaxies look like globes of light. They could have anywhere between 100 million and 100 trillion stars in them.

4  Irregular galaxies don't have a clear shape or structure. They look like blobs of stars and are usually smaller than the other types of galaxies.

5 Spiral galaxies look like flat pinwheels. They have a bright bulge of stars near the center and often a black hole.

25 STARRY FACTS ABOUT

6 Some spiral galaxies have stars that line up like a bright bar through their centers. These are called barred spiral galaxies.

7 THE MILKY WAY IS THE GALAXY WE LIVE IN. ALTHOUGH WE CANNOT SEE IT FROM THE OUTSIDE, MOST ASTRONOMERS THINK IT IS A BARRED SPIRAL.

8 The Milky Way has between 200 and 400 billion stars. Most of the stars are near the center, while others are clumped near one another to form spiral arms.

9 The spiral arms of the Milky Way span about 100,000 light-years from end to end. But our galaxy also includes a halo of dust and gas that extends even farther.

10 The Andromeda galaxy is the closest spiral galaxy to the Milky Way. It is about 2.5 million light-years away.

11 With about a trillion stars, the Andromeda galaxy is also the largest galaxy in our galactic neighborhood, often called the Local Group of galaxies.

12  The hatlike Sombrero galaxy is a flat disk of billions of stars. From our view, we can see the "hat's" edge clearly, with dark dust lanes cutting through it.

13

In a dark sky, the Andromeda galaxy is visible without a telescope. That makes it **the farthest thing you can see with the naked eye.**

14 Galaxies move through space, and **they can run into one another.** Over millions of years, these galactic collisions can change the galaxies' shapes dramatically.

16

M51, known as the **Whirlpool galaxy,** is **actually two galaxies:** a larger spiral galaxy tugged by a smaller galaxy passing by.

15

The Milky Way and Andromeda galaxies are on **a collision course.** They will run into each other in about **4.5 billion years.**

17 THE WORD "GALAXY" COMES FROM THE GREEK WORD FOR MILK. IN THE SKY, THE MILKY WAY LOOKS A LITTLE LIKE SPILLED MILK.

GALAXIES

18 The elliptical galaxy **M87** is one of the **biggest galaxies** around. Astronomers think the stars in this galaxy weigh as much as 2.4 trillion suns.

19 The **farthest** galaxy that astronomers have seen may be **GN-z11.** It is about 13.4 billion light-years from Earth.

20 Most of the galaxies in the universe are **much smaller** than the Milky Way. Astronomers call them **dwarf galaxies.**

21 The closest galaxy to the Milky Way is **Canis Major Dwarf.** It is so near to us that the gravitational pull of our Milky Way is **ripping away its stars.**

22 From Earth's Southern Hemisphere, you can see **two dwarf galaxies** without a telescope. These are called the **Large Magellanic Clouds** and the **Small Magellanic Clouds.**

23 For a long time, astronomers thought the Magellanic Clouds circled the Milky Way like moons. But now we see that they are really **moving fast past our galaxy.** They will eventually fly away from us.

24 ASTRONOMERS HAVE OBSERVED MILLIONS OF GALAXIES BUT HAVE **NAMED ONLY A FEW.** MOST ARE GIVEN **COMBINATIONS OF LETTERS AND NUMBERS** LIKE M100 OR NGC 3310.

25 Based on recent sky surveys, up to two trillion galaxies may be in our universe.

1 Exoplanets (also called extrasolar planets) are **worlds that orbit stars** beyond our sun and solar system.

2 Astronomers have discovered **more than 4,000** exoplanets in our galaxy. More than 5,000 exoplanet candidates—planets that aren't yet confirmed—await further study.

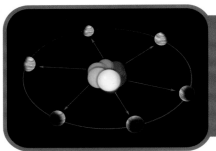

3 Exoplanets are so far away and so close to their bright stars that they are **extremely difficult to see in a telescope.** Instead, astronomers look for stars that "**wobble,**" which means a big planet might be tugging on them.

4 The most successful way to find exoplanets is the **transit method:** noticing when a planet regularly **goes in front of the star** and blocks some of its light.

5 Exoplanets larger than Jupiter that **orbit very close to their stars** are called "**hot Jupiters.**"

6 **HD 114762 b** is an exoplanet **11 times more massive than Jupiter.** It is so huge that when astronomers first saw it, they thought it was a brown dwarf star.

7 Exoplanet **51 Pegasi b** is about half the size of Jupiter. The exoplanet is so close to its star that it circles it **once every four days.**

Artist's idea of exoplanet TRAPPIST-1f

FACTS ABOUT EXOPLANETS

8 Scientists used a (now retired) space telescope called Kepler to discover thousands of exoplanets. A new mission named TESS (Transiting Exoplanets Survey Satellite) is continuing the search.

9 Kepler-16b was the first exoplanet found to circle a double star. That means if you lived there, you would have two suns in your sky.

10 CoRoT-7b was the first super-Earth (a rocky exoplanet larger than Earth) to be discovered. But CoRoT-7b is so close to its star that it may be about 2000°F (1093°C) on its surface.

11 The Kepler-90 star has eight planets, like our solar system. Also like in our solar system, the planets closer to the star are smaller and rocky, whereas the ones farther out are large and gaseous.

12 Astronomers call the area of a solar system that is not too hot and not too cold the "Goldilocks zone" (also known as the "habitable zone"). Exoplanets found here are at just the right distance from their star and could support life as we know it.

13 The exoplanet closest to Earth's size may be Kepler-1649c. It is only slightly larger than Earth and orbits in the habitable zone of a red dwarf star.

14 TRAPPIST-1 is a star system 40 light-years away with at least seven planets. Three of them may be in the Goldilocks zone, which provides three more places to look for life.

15 Exoplanet Kepler-22b may have an ocean of liquid water covering its surface. If so, the surface temperature could be a mild 60°F (16°C).

75 TWINKLING FACTS ABOUT STARS

1 Stars are enormous balls of gas. They make their own heat and light through fusion—the combining of elements, which produces a lot of energy.

2 Most stars are spherical (round) because of the intense gravity pulling their gas and other materials toward their center.

3 Gases may seem weightless, but anything with mass has gravity. The gravity of stars is so intense that they cause nearby planets to circle them.

4 Although most stars look white to the unaided eye, stars come in many different colors, including red, orange, yellow, white, and blue.

5 A star's color can tell astronomers its temperature. Reddish stars are cooler, yellow stars are in the middle, and bluer stars are the hottest.

6 Stars come in all different sizes. They include dwarfs that are a few thousand miles or kilometers across and supergiants that can be more than 600 million miles (966 million km) wide.

7 Distances to stars are measured in light-years: the distance that light can travel in one year.

8 THE FARTHEST STARS YOU CAN SEE WITH THE NAKED EYE ARE THOUSANDS OF LIGHT-YEARS AWAY.

9 Astronomers could not measure the distance to any star until 1838. That year, German astronomer Friedrich Bessel measured the motion of the star 61 Cygni and proved it was about 11 light-years from Earth.

10 Astronomers measure the brightness of things in space using "magnitude." First-magnitude stars are the brightest, second-magnitude stars are second brightest, and so on.

11 ASTRONOMERS GIVE EVERY OBJECT IN SPACE AN ADDRESS. THEY PLOT OUT EVERY STAR ON DETAILED STAR CHARTS.

12 Stars twinkle because their light travels trillions of miles or kilometers through space. The small amount of starlight that finally reaches Earth is easily scattered by our atmosphere.

13 Generations of stargazers have looked upon the same sky. The stars and star patterns they identified have not changed significantly in thousands of years.

14 In the Middle Ages, great Arab astronomers named most of the bright and visible stars, such as Betelgeuse (BEETLE-juice), Aldebaran, and Deneb.

15 Other star names, like Sirius, Castor, and Pollux, are more than 2,000 years old and come from ancient Greek astronomers.

16 Ancient Babylonians and Assyrians named Nunki, a star in the constellation Sagittarius. It may be the oldest star name still in use.

17 Two stars in the constellation Libra—Zubenelgenubi (zoo-BEN-el-je-NEW-bee) and Zubeneschamali (zoo-BEN-ess-sha-MA-lee)—mean "southern claw" and "northern claw" because some cultures saw them as part of a scorpion.

18 The star name Antares comes from Greek words that mean "the rival of Mars." That's because Antares has a reddish color similar to the red planet, and the two objects can regularly be seen close together.

19 The North Star is also known as Polaris. Because it lies nearly above Earth's North Pole, it does not seem to move over the course of a night. It is a year-round landmark in the northern sky.

20 The North Star is not the brightest star in the sky. It actually ranks about 50th among all the stars you can see from Earth.

21 Earth's axis wobbles a little over centuries, pointing the North Pole at different parts of the sky. So thousands of years ago, the star Thuban in the constellation Draco (the Dragon) was the north star instead of Polaris.

22 YOU CAN NEVER SEE THE NORTH STAR IN THE SKY FROM THE SOUTHERN HEMISPHERE.

23 The Southern Hemisphere does not have an equally bright and notable star marking the southern sky. There is no "South Star."

24 Aldebaran is a red giant star 65 light-years away that marks the eye of the constellation Taurus (the Bull).

25 Betelgeuse is a red, supergiant star about 870 million miles (1.4 billion km) wide.

26 If our sun were the size of Betelgeuse, the planets Mercury, Venus, Earth, Mars, and Jupiter would orbit inside it and burn up.

27 Spots on the surface of the star Betelgeuse resemble sunspots on the sun. If you had to name them, you might call them "Betel-spots."

28 Betelgeuse is only about 10 million years old—young for a star—but because it is so large, it ages rapidly. It could soon explode in a supernova. ("Soon" to astronomers is within the next 10,000 years.)

29 Orion's brightest star is Rigel, which means "left foot." This blue supergiant gives off nearly 363,000 times the light of our sun.

30 Orion's shoulder star is Bellatrix, which means "beautiful warrior woman." Bellatrix is deep blue and lies 240 light-years from Earth.

31 The stars of Orion's belt are named Alnitak, Alnilam, and Mintaka. These can be translated to mean "the girdle," "the string of pearls," and simply "the belt."

32 SIRIUS IS THE BRIGHTEST STAR VISIBLE AT NIGHT.

33 Sirius is one of the closest stars to the sun. It is only about 8.6 light-years or 50 million miles (80.5 million km) away.

34 Sirius is known as the "Dog Star," because it marks the nose of the constellation Canis Major (Big Dog).

The Milky Way among other stars

35 The constellation Canis Minor (Little Dog) has a bright star too. It's called Procyon, which means "before the dog," because it rises in the eastern sky just before Sirius.

36 Both dog stars, Sirius and Procyon, are double stars. Each has a small white dwarf star circling the main star.

37 Most of the stars you see in the night sky are not just one star. They might look like one star to the naked eye, but they usually consist of two, three, or more stars orbiting one another.

38 The two stars in the Albireo system are different colors and brightnesses. In a telescope you can see a dim blue star next to a brighter orange star.

39 Capella is the brightest star in the constellation Auriga. The light you see comes from at least four stars circling one another: two yellow stars and two red ones.

40 Castor looks like one star to the naked eye, but it is actually a system of six stars circling one another.

42 Nu Scorpii and AR Cassiopeiae are septuple stars—seven stars that orbit a common center. With so many suns in the sky, any aliens living around these stars would never experience darkness.

43 Almost every star you see in the night sky with the naked eye is larger than the sun.

44 Altair, which marks the eagle eye in the constellation Aquila (Eagle), spins once every nine hours. This rapid rotation squishes the star into an egg shape.

45 According to astronomers there are no green stars. Humans' eyes can see red, orange, yellow, white, and blue in the stars, but not green.

46 Fomalhaut means "fish's mouth." It is the brightest star in the constellation Piscis Austrinus (Southern Fish).

47 Some types of stars, called variable stars, change their brightness regularly. If our sun were a variable star, it would be bright one year and dim the next.

48 The variable star Algol is actually two stars that circle each other. When one star moves in front of the other, Algol dims dramatically. Ancient stargazers were afraid of this winking star.

49 Algol has many scary nicknames around the world, including "the Ghoul," "Medusa's Head," "Demon Star," and "Piled-Up Corpses."

50 OUT IN THE COUNTRYSIDE AND UNDER THE DARKEST SKIES, YOU CAN SEE 2,000 TO 2,500 STARS IN THE SKY AT ONE TIME.

51 Various groups in the ancient world tested their eyesight using the double stars Mizar and Alcor in the Big Dipper. If you could see them both with the naked eye, you could be a scout or a hunter.

52 Mizar and Alcor have many nicknames around the world, including "the Horse and Rider," "the Apron," and "the Forgotten."

53 Beta Pictoris is a very young star at only about 12 million years old. Around it, astronomers found a dusty disk of material that could hold the building blocks of future planets.

54 One star in the constellation Cetus (Sea Monster) is rarely visible to the naked eye. But about every 332 days, it brightens enough to be seen. Ancient astronomers named it Mira, "the wonderful."

55 No one is sure why Mira changes its brightness so much, but during one flare-up it became 1,500 times brighter than normal.

56 Mira flies through space at about 81 miles (130 km) a second, leaving a trail of gas behind it that is now 13 light-years long.

57 Every 27 years the star Epsilon Aurigae dims by about half. Astronomers think that happens when a doughnut-shaped cloud of dark material comes between us and the star.

58 P Cygni is one of the most luminous (bright) stars in our galaxy. But at 5,500 light-years away, it cannot be seen without a telescope.

59 Arcturus is the fourth brightest star in the sky. Its name means "Guardian of the Bear," because it follows the constellation Ursa Major (Big Bear) around the night sky.

60 Barnard's Star shifts its position in the sky faster than any other star visible from Earth. It still takes hundreds of years for any change to be significant enough to notice.

61 Astronomers nicknamed HD 140283 the "Methuselah star" after a very old man in the Hebrew Bible, because the star may be the most ancient ever seen—more than 13 billion years old.

62 Alphecca is the brightest star in the constellation Corona Borealis (Northern Crown). Many ancient cultures saw it as the crown's brightest jewel.

63 A "ZOMBIE STAR" IS A STAR WITHIN A STAR. WHEN A SMALL NEUTRON STAR COLLIDES WITH A HUMONGOUS RED STAR, IT CAN BE ABSORBED AND STILL CONTINUE TO EXIST.

64 Astronomers estimate that about one septillion (1,000,000,000,000,000,000,000,000) stars could be in the observable universe.

65 Proxima Centauri is the closest star to Earth (other than the sun). It is about 4.24 light-years away, or 25 trillion miles (40 trillion km).

66 Proxima Centauri is a red dwarf star that circles two other larger, yellow-white stars in the Alpha Centauri system.

67 Proxima Centauri has only 12 percent the mass of our sun and is only 124,000 miles (200,000 km) in diameter.

68 Astronomers have discovered at least one planet within the Alpha Centauri system, making that world the closest planet to the eight in our solar system.

69 Deneb, the tail star of the constellation Cygnus (Swan), is one of the farthest single stars you can see without a telescope. Astronomers estimate Deneb to be between 1,500 and 3,200 light-years away.

70 THE HOTTEST KNOWN STAR, WR 102, MAY HAVE A SURFACE TEMPERATURE OF 378,000°F (210,000°C), ABOUT 38 TIMES HOTTER THAN THE SURFACE OF OUR SUN.

71 The coldest star may be tiny WISE 0855-0714, at minus 8° to minus 54°F (-22 to -48°C)—colder than ice. Astronomers are currently debating if it is a star or something else, such as a gas giant planet.

72 The stars Shaula and Lesath mark the stinger of the constellation Scorpius (Scorpion). They appear so close together that they have inspired the nickname of the Cat's Eyes.

73 There are no frog constellations, but the star Diphda has a mysterious nickname. Arabic astronomers called it the Second Frog. Why? No one knows.

74 Regulus is the brightest star in the constellation Leo. Regulus means "little king," because it marks the heart of the lion constellation—and the lion is the king of the beasts.

75 For a fee, many private companies will let you name a star. However, these names are not official. The only official group that can name things in space is the International Astronomical Union (IAU).

1 Stars are created by humongous clouds of gas and dust called **nebulae.**

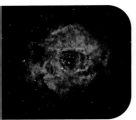

2 **Gravity** brings the gas and dust together across vast distances in space. Heat and pressure build up in the cloud until a **protostar**—a very hot clump of gas—forms at the center.

3 A star is born when the gases in the protostar's core begin **fusion.** The hydrogen gas in the core is under such heat and pressure that it **turns into helium** and releases a tremendous amount of energy.

4 Sometimes a **nebula's gases** are spinning so quickly that **two, three, or more stars** can form from the same cloud.

5 Not all the matter in a nebula forms into a star or stars. **Leftover pieces can come together** at various distances to make planets, **asteroids,** moons, and comets.

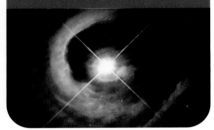

25 EXPLOSIVE
FACTS ABOUT THE

6 TELESCOPES HAVE CAPTURED IMAGES OF **PROTOSTARS, NEWBORN STARS,** AND **DISKS OF MATERIAL** THAT COULD FORM INTO SOLAR SYSTEMS IN THE **ORION NEBULA,** A HUGE CLOUD OF GAS LOCATED IN THE CONSTELLATION **ORION.**

7 A star is **most stable** when the force of gravity trying to crush it inward equals the explosive **nuclear energy** pushing outward from its center.

8 The **life span** and ultimate death of a star depend almost completely on its mass. **The bigger the star, the shorter its life** and the more dramatic its demise will be.

9 **Small stars** can live between 100 billion and a trillion years. Because the universe is about 13.8 billion years old, **astronomers have never seen a small star die.**

10 About **90 percent** of the stars in our part of the galaxy get their energy by **turning hydrogen into helium** deep within the stars.

11 Stars like **our sun** are **midsize.** They take about 50 million years to form and **can live for about 10 billion years.**

13

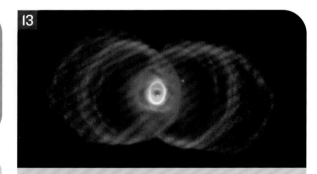

12

At the end of its life, a star like the sun will eventually **cool and turn orange and then red.** During this **red giant stage,** it will expand until it is several times bigger than it used to be.

After billions of years a red giant star will not be able to hold itself together. Its outer shells will **blast into outer space** and create a huge ring of material called a **planetary nebula.**

14 After a planetary nebula expands into space, what remains of the star will change into a small, dense star called a **white dwarf.**

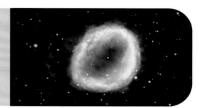

15 If a white dwarf is circling near another star, **it can steal gas from that star,** triggering another type of explosion called a **nova.** (This is not the same as a supernova!)

16 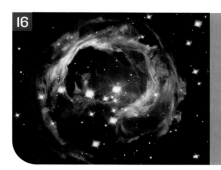 **Supergiant stars** that are much more massive than our sun **use up their fuel so fast** that they live for only millions of years, rather than billions.

17 When a supergiant star dies, its core **collapses and then bounces back out.** This tremendous explosion is called a **supernova.**

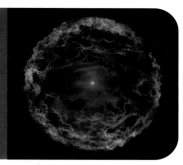

LIFE AND DEATH OF STARS

18 About two or three supernovas happen **in our Milky Way galaxy every 100 years.** But astronomers can observe supernovas happening in other galaxies far, far away.

19 If a star is massive enough and enough material is left over after a supernova, its core can collapse to form a **neutron star** or even a **black hole**—a spot of gravity so intense not even light can escape.

20 A neutron star can be only 12 miles (19 km) wide, but it would be so dense that **a piece the size of a sugar cube would weigh as much as Mount Everest.**

21 The **leftover parts of a supernova explosion** are called **remnants.** They can spread out across more than 100 light-years of space— **about 20 times the distance from our sun to the nearest star.**

22 Supernova remnants fly through space and eventually **mingle with parts of other exploded stars.** When enough of these parts come together, they will create **new star-forming nebulae.**

23 THE HEAT AND PRESSURE OF SUPERNOVAS CREATE **HEAVY ELEMENTS** THAT ARE ESSENTIAL TO LIFE. THESE INCLUDE **NITROGEN, OXYGEN, AND IRON.**

24 The air in your lungs and **the iron in your blood** can have come from only one place: **a tremendous supernova.** A long time ago a massive star exploded and created these elements, which eventually became part of our solar system, our planet, **and our bodies.**

25 If you go back in time far enough, each and every part of you was once **inside a really gigantic star.** You and everyone you know are truly **SUPERSTARS!**

1 Ancient stargazers around the world marveled at the stars in the sky. Almost every culture connected the stars into shapes, patterns, people, and animals. We call these star shapes constellations.

2 Making up stories about the constellations was so popular that these starry legends have been passed down from generation to generation for thousands of years.

3 A 17,000-year-old cave painting in Lascaux, France, portrays the constellation Taurus (the Bull). It comes complete with an accurate drawing of the Seven Sisters star cluster above the bull's back.

4 Starting in 1922, an international group of astronomers agreed to recognize 88 official constellations. Most were first documented thousands of years ago and come from stories in ancient Greek mythology.

5 Some constellations used before 1922 did not make it into the final 88 and are not used anymore, including Noctua (the Owl), Vespa (the Wasp), and Cerberus (the Three-Headed Dog).

25 MYTHOLOGICAL FACTS ABOUT

6 Constellations near the sky's north or south poles can be seen every night. However, other constellations are best seen in different seasons and are called seasonal constellations.

7 Your view of the stars changes as you travel north or south. Stargazers in the Southern Hemisphere can see many stars and constellations not visible from the Northern Hemisphere.

8 The path that the planets, sun, and moon regularly travel through the sky passes through 12 constellations. Known as the zodiac, these constellations helped ancient people keep track of important times of the year.

9 The 12 zodiac constellations are Aries (Ram), Taurus (Bull), Gemini (Twins), Cancer (Crab), Leo (Lion), Virgo (Maiden), Libra (Scales), Scorpius (Scorpion), Sagittarius (Archer), Capricornus (Sea Goat), Aquarius (Water Bearer), and Pisces (Fish).

10 The Hydra (Water Snake) is the largest constellation and coils across the sky every spring. From its seven heads to its tail, Hydra spans more than a quarter of the way around the sky.

11 According to legend, the hero Hercules (who became a constellation) killed three creatures that also became constellations: Hydra (by lopping off its heads), Leo (by strangling it), and Cancer (by squishing it under his heel).

12 THE BIG DIPPER AND LITTLE DIPPER ARE NOT OFFICIAL CONSTELLATIONS. THEY ARE ASTERISMS, UNOFFICIAL PARTS OF LARGER CONSTELLATIONS.

13

The Big Dipper is actually part of **Ursa Major** (Great Bear), and the Little Dipper is part of **Ursa Minor** (Little Bear).

14 To the ancient Greeks, the stars in **Scorpius** formed the outline of a menacing scorpion. But in Hawaiian folklore the constellation was known as **Maui's Fishhook** because of its distinct curved pattern of stars.

15 French astronomer Nicolas-Louis de Lacaille added the **newest** of the 88 official constellations in the 1700s. He connected the stars to honor impressive inventions of his day, such as the **telescope**, **microscope**, and **clock**.

16 **Delphinus** (the Dolphin) is one of the **smallest constellations** in the sky. It looks a little like a dolphin arching its back and jumping above the cosmic waves.

17 The smallest constellation is **Crux, the Southern Cross,** visible mainly in the Southern Hemisphere. The Maori people of New Zealand called these stars **"the Anchor,"** while the ancient Inca of Peru saw them as **"the Stair."**

18 **SAGITTARIUS** is known as the Archer, but ancient Greeks saw it as **a centaur**—a creature of mythology that was half human, half horse—who is also wielding **a bow and arrow.**

CONSTELLATIONS

19 **Orion** (the Hunter) is the most famous and easy-to-recognize constellation. Orion sports **a belt** of three stars in a row, with additional bright stars marking his feet and shoulders.

20 Corona Borealis is officially known as the **Northern Crown,** but Australian Aboriginals see this semicircle of seven stars as a **boomerang** flying through the heavens.

21

The outline of the long and skinny constellation **Draco** (the Dragon) definitely resembles a serpent. In an ancient Babylonian myth, these stars are Tiamat the she-dragon, who battles the god **Marduk** for mastery of all creation.

22 **THE TWINS** that make up Gemini include the two bright stars **Pollux and Castor.** In African mythology, these stars were known as the Wise and Foolish Antelopes. Other cultures called them the Two Peacocks, the Two Kids, or the Giant's Eyes.

23 **Cygnus** (the Swan) is an easy constellation to find on nights from July to November. Its stars form a **long cross shape,** so it has the nickname of the Northern Cross.

24

IN GREEK MYTHOLOGY, **CASSIOPEIA** THE QUEEN WAS KNOWN FOR BRAGGING ABOUT HER BEAUTY. THE STARS IN HER CONSTELLATION LOOK LIKE THE LETTER W, AND SHE SITS IN THE SKY **UPSIDE DOWN** AS A PUNISHMENT FOR HER VANITY.

25 On January and February evenings, you can see **a dramatic scene in the stars:** Orion fends off Taurus (the Bull) while his two hunting dogs (Canis Major and Canis Minor) try to help.

1  Far beyond our solar system lie massive **collections of stars and gases** such as star clusters, nebulae, and galaxies. These are called **deep-space objects.**

2 In the 18th century, French astronomer **Charles Messier** created a **catalog** of 110 deep-space objects that he saw in his telescope.

3 Messier's objects, all **labeled with the letter M,** include some of the night sky's most impressive deep-space sights. They are famously **good targets** for beginning sky-watchers to find in telescopes.

4 Every March and April, around a new moon, it is possible to find **all 110 M objects in one night.** Sky-watchers call this a **Messier marathon.**

5  In the constellation Orion you can find **M42, the Orion Nebula,** a huge star-forming region. Even though it is almost 1,500 light-years away, **you can see it without a telescope.**

25 FARAWAY FACTS ABOUT

6 Three kinds of nebulae combine to make **M20,** or the **Trifid Nebula.** It looks like a three-petaled flower made of light.

7 One of the most famous images in astronomy is a close-up of one section of M16, the **Eagle Nebula.** Called the Pillars of Creation, this region's towers of dust and gas hold **countless newborn stars.**

8 Two thousand light-years away is M57, the **Ring Nebula.** Astronomers can peer inside this ring of expanding gas to **the tiny star** in the center.

11 The constellation Taurus holds M1, or the **Crab Nebula,** the gas and dust remaining from a supernova explosion in **1054.** At its center lies the Crab Pulsar, a bright neutron star.

9 The **Dumbbell Nebula** (M27) was the first planetary nebula ever discovered. A single star couldn't hold itself together, so *poof*—the outer shells of the star **blasted** away to form a beautiful pattern.

10 THE **HELIX NEBULA** SHOWS THE SHOCK WAVE FROM A DYING STAR. IT LOOKS LIKE **AN EYEBALL** STARING BACK AT YOU.

12 The last really dramatic **supernova** to be seen from Earth happened in 1604. Then, a star suddenly became **brighter than any other star in the sky.**

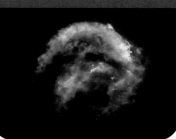

13 Clusters of stars light up two huge pockets of gases in the constellation **Cassiopeia.** One looks like a human heart and is called the **Heart Nebula;** the other is called the **Soul Nebula.**

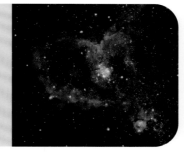

14 The **Horsehead Nebula** is a favorite subject of astronomy photos. It looks like a **black stallion** in front of a sea of pinkish gas.

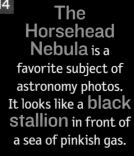

15 A star cloud near the constellation Cygnus looks exactly like a **continent.** It's called the **North America Nebula.**

16 SOMETIMES STARS ARE FOUND IN CLUMPS, BOUND TOGETHER BY GRAVITY. SMALLER CLUMPS OFTEN HAVE A LITTLE MORE OPEN SPACE BETWEEN THE STARS. THESE ARE CALLED OPEN CLUSTERS.

17 The Pleiades, also known as **the Seven Sisters,** is one of the most famous **open star clusters.** You can find it near the constellation Taurus (the Bull).

DEEP-SPACE OBJECTS

18 At first glance **the Pleiades** cluster looks like **a cloud.** When you peer deeper, you can see some of the stars in the cluster.

19 If you look carefully at the constellation Taurus, you may notice several **EXTRA STARS** near the bright star Aldebaran. They are part of **THE HYADES,** the closest open cluster to our solar system.

20 **M6,** an open star cluster near Scorpius (the Scorpion), is called the **Butterfly cluster** because it looks a little like a butterfly of stars.

21 Larger clumps of stars, called **globular clusters,** look like glowing globes through a small telescope. When you look at a globular cluster, you are seeing the light of hundreds of thousands of stars.

22

Globular clusters are some of the **largest and oldest structures** in the Milky Way. Within our galaxy, some globular clusters contain stars that are **12 billion years old.**

23 One of the biggest and brightest globular clusters is called M13, or **the Hercules cluster.** It has about **300,000 stars** stretching across almost 150 light-years of our galaxy.

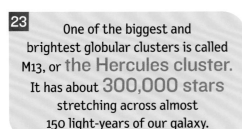

24 **Omega Centauri** is the largest globular cluster in the Milky Way galaxy. It is 17,000 light-years away and includes **millions of stars.**

25 Recently astronomers found a **medium-size black hole** in the center of Omega Centauri. Some astronomers think Omega Centauri may actually be a small **galaxy** inside our Milky Way galaxy instead of a globular cluster.

15 FANCIFUL FACTS ABOUT UFOs,

1 Even the best astronomers don't always get things right. Before the 1500s, almost all astronomers believed that the sun orbited Earth.

2 If you have an irrational fear of the universe—like the belief that the sun will kill us, Earth will stop spinning, or a black hole will swallow us up—you suffer from cosmophobia.

3 Some people believed Halley's comet would kill people with poisonous gas when it flew by in 1910. And others believed comet Elenin would crash into Earth in 2011. Neither disaster happened.

4 Some people call a lunar eclipse a "Blood Moon" to make it sound scarier. But Blood Moons look red only because our atmosphere is scattering the moonlight. They have no long-lasting effect on Earth and do not signal the end of the world.

5 In the 1800s, many astronomers thoroughly searched for another planet closer to the sun than Mercury, nicknamed Vulcan. Modern astronomers know that Vulcan does not exist.

6 In 1600, an Italian friar named Giordano Bruno was burned at the stake for saying (correctly) that Earth went around the sun, and that the universe was infinite.

7 Astronomy and astrology are very different. Astronomy is the scientific study of outer space, whereas astrology unscientifically uses star charts to try to predict the future.

Artist's idea of a collision in space

DOOMSDAYS, AND OTHER URBAN LEGENDS

8 The **SETI** (Search for Extraterrestrial Intelligence) Institute is a team effort of scientists around the world who **hope to detect alien life in outer space.**

9 In the 1950s, Italian physicist Enrico Fermi posed the question, "Where are they?" This is called the Fermi paradox: Our galaxy alone has billions of stars, many with planets, but we haven't seen one example of alien life.

10 The misreading of ancient Maya mythology made many people believe the world would end when one cycle of the Maya calendar ended in 2012. That, of course, didn't happen.

11 In 1947 in Roswell, New Mexico, U.S.A., a high-tech balloon crashed. The wreckage looked so strange that a lot of people thought it was a flying saucer.

12 The planet Venus is so suspiciously bright in the nighttime sky that people often mistake it for a UFO.

13 When you take a picture of the night sky with your cell phone camera, you often get artifacts—extra blips of light or duplicate images. They are not UFOs, but are instead created by your camera as it focuses.

14 Despite the saying "It must be a full moon," there is no connection between full moons and crime, births, deaths, or widespread behavior in humans.

15 Some people predicted the end of the world would happen on September 23, 2017, when several planets appeared together in the sky around the constellation Virgo. It had no effect on Earth at all.

❶ **Space is big!** When you see a planet in the night sky, it is millions of miles away. A star is trillions of miles from you. And galaxies are **millions of trillions of miles away.**

❷ Most human-made satellites travel at about 17,000 miles an hour (27,359 km/h), which means they can **circle Earth in about 90 minutes.** If a school bus traveled at that speed, it would get you to school in seconds.

❸ The farthest distance humans have ever traveled is to an orbit around **the far side of the moon. Apollo 13** astronauts reached this spot, **248,655 miles** (400,171 km) from Earth, in 1970.

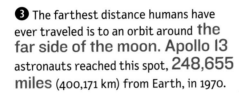

❹ **Missions from Earth to Mars** can launch every 26 months, when the two planets are closer to each other. **A trip to the red planet takes five to 10 months** to fly the tens of millions of miles.

❺ Astronomers typically use the astronomical unit, or AU, when measuring distances within the solar system. **An AU is the average distance from Earth to the sun,** equal to about 93 million miles (150 million km).

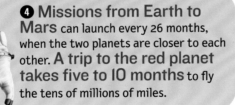

❻ The farthest object ever visited by a spacecraft is a **tiny, icy object called Arrokoth.** It took the New Horizons spacecraft 13 years to reach it, **billions of miles away** in the outer reaches of the solar system.

❼ The farthest known object in our solar system is nicknamed **FarFarOut.** It is 140 astronomical units from the sun, or **13 billion miles** (21 billion km) away.

Photographing starlight

64

SPACE AND TIME

❽ Light speed is the speed at which light travels—more than 186,000 miles (300,000 km) a second. So light can travel from Earth to the moon in 1.25 seconds and **from Earth to Neptune in 4.2 hours.**

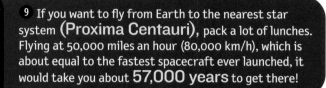

9 If you want to fly from Earth to the nearest star system **(Proxima Centauri)**, pack a lot of lunches. Flying at 50,000 miles an hour (80,000 km/h), which is about equal to the fastest spacecraft ever launched, it would take you about **57,000 years** to get there!

❿ One light-year is the distance light can travel in one year. That is equal to about 5,880,000,000,000 miles (9,460,000,000,000 km).

⓫ It takes **years** for light to travel **from stars to Earth.** If a star is 100 light-years away, the twinkling light just now reaching your eyes left that star **100 years ago.**

⓬ Driving a Mars rover from Earth is tricky because, even traveling at the speed of light, it takes between **4 and 24 minutes to send a signal to it**—and another 4 to 24 minutes to get a response.

⓭ You can see the **Andromeda galaxy** with your naked eye. That means you are seeing something without a telescope that is 2.5 million light-years—or about **15 quintillion miles** (24 quintillion km)—away!

⓮ Physics tells us that if you rocketed off Earth and traveled close to the speed of light, **you would age more slowly than the people you left behind.** If you had a twin sister, when you returned home, she would be older than you.

⓯ The science of astronomy can sound like science fiction. **Time machines** have not been invented yet, but if you could somehow travel faster than the speed of light, **you would literally go backward in time.**

15 WINDY FACTS ABOUT

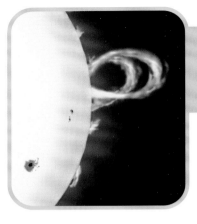

❶ Activity on the sun, such as **solar flares**, creates weather in space. These solar storms can even **reach the planets.**

❷ The sun **shoots particles** into space at about one million miles an hour (1.6 million km/h). This is called the **solar wind.**

3 Even though the **solar wind** travels so fast, when a blast of energy leaves the sun, it still takes **two to four days** to reach Earth.

❹ Especially violent **sun storms** directed at Earth can damage satellites, **mess up cell phone signals,** and overload power lines.

❺ **Mercury does not have seasons** like those on Earth. The planet is barely tilted and spins so slowly that temperatures are the same every day.

❻ **Venus has some of the strongest winds** of any rocky planet. Some storms that rage high in the air can reach 225 miles an hour (362 km/h).

❼ The dense clouds on Venus don't rain water: **They rain sulfuric acid.** Most of this acid rain probably evaporates before hitting the ground.

❽ **Mars has snow** at its north and south poles. Scientists aren't sure if it falls from the sky or just **forms on the ground out of the thin air.**

Artist's idea of lightning on Venus

WEATHER IN SPACE

9 More than a dozen **cyclones swirl around the south pole of Jupiter.** Some of these storms are **600 miles** (965 km) wide.

10 **Jupiter and Saturn** likely have **diamonds floating in their clouds.** Some of them may fall like rain and sink into the planets.

11 **Neptune's winds** move with incredible speed. One white cloud of gas moved across the surface so fast that astronomers nicknamed it **"Scooter."**

12 An exoplanet (a planet orbiting another star) named **HD 189733b** has **bright blue skies.** But winds there gust at 4,500 miles an hour (7,242 km/h), and **it rains glass instead of water.**

13 Exoplanet **Kepler-10b** orbits a star 564 light-years away. On the side that always faces its sun, temperatures on this world could reach **2840°F** (1560°C).

14 Exoplanet **55 Cancri e** circles so close to its star that it may be **covered in lava.** The surface of this exoplanet could be about **4900°F** (2704°C).

15 Exoplanet **HAT-P-7b** has clouds made of corundum. On Earth, this mineral helps form **rubies and sapphires.**

15 GRIPPING FACTS

1 A **black hole** is a place in space where gravity is so intense that **nothing can escape it, not even light.**

2 Because no one can see inside a black hole, **no one knows for sure what happens** to anything that falls into it.

3 A black hole is not empty space. It is actually **a whole lot of matter jammed into a really small area** to create a superdense object.

4 **All the mass** of a black hole can be found at a point in the center called **the singularity.**

5 Our own galaxy has a **supermassive black hole** in the center called **Sagittarius A*** (pronounced A star). It may contain **4.3 million times the mass of the sun.**

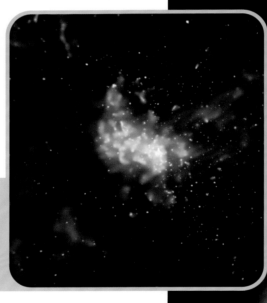

6 Because black holes don't give off any light, they are **invisible through normal telescopes.** Astronomers detect them by looking for **x-rays** shooting out of them or by watching objects circle an empty-looking area.

7 In 2019, a team of scientists **coordinated eight radio telescopes around the world** to work as a single massive telescope so they could capture **the first ever image of a black hole**—at the center of galaxy M87.

Artist's idea of a black hole

ABOUT BLACK HOLES

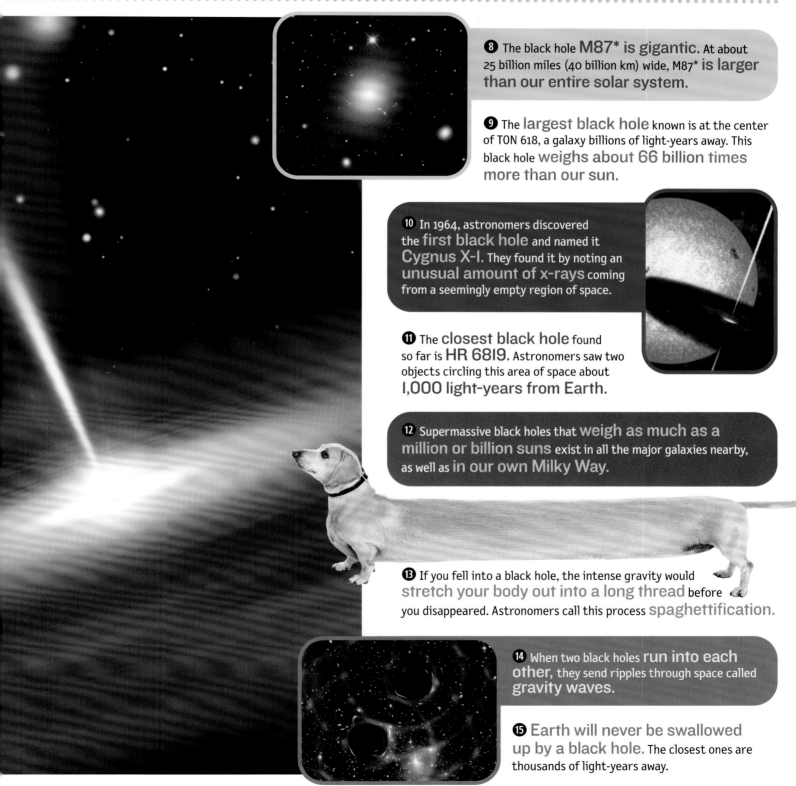

8 The black hole M87* is gigantic. At about 25 billion miles (40 billion km) wide, M87* is larger than our entire solar system.

9 The largest black hole known is at the center of TON 618, a galaxy billions of light-years away. This black hole weighs about 66 billion times more than our sun.

10 In 1964, astronomers discovered the first black hole and named it Cygnus X-I. They found it by noting an unusual amount of x-rays coming from a seemingly empty region of space.

11 The closest black hole found so far is HR 6819. Astronomers saw two objects circling this area of space about 1,000 light-years from Earth.

12 Supermassive black holes that weigh as much as a million or billion suns exist in all the major galaxies nearby, as well as in our own Milky Way.

13 If you fell into a black hole, the intense gravity would stretch your body out into a long thread before you disappeared. Astronomers call this process spaghettification.

14 When two black holes run into each other, they send ripples through space called gravity waves.

15 Earth will never be swallowed up by a black hole. The closest ones are thousands of light-years away.

1 When orbiting Earth in the INTERNATIONAL SPACE STATION (ISS), astronauts travel at 18,000 miles an hour (29,000 km/h).

2 ISS astronauts fly 432,000 miles (695,000 km) EVERY DAY and about 157,788,000 miles (254,000,000 km) IN A YEAR.

3 When a spacecraft is out of direct sunlight, the craft is SO COLD that it needs heaters to keep it from FREEZING.

9 In the 1960s, space food was so yucky that John Young SMUGGLED IN A CORNED BEEF SANDWICH in his space suit.

10 In 1978, Soviet astronaut Aleksandr Ivanchenkov found a BOX OF CHOCOLATES his wife had sent with the supplies.

11 Astronauts don't eat meals at a table. They must strap themselves to a wall or EAT WHILE FLOATING.

17 For liftoffs, space walks, and landings, astronauts wear Maximum Absorbency Garments (MAGs)—SPACE DIAPERS.

18 On the ISS, astronauts' PEE is purified and recycled into fresh, clean DRINKING WATER.

23 Some astronauts LOSE THEIR SENSE OF DIRECTION because there is no up or down in microgravity.

24 If you need A HAIRCUT on the ISS, you use electric clippers, which are attached to a vacuum that sucks up loose hair.

29 After their work is done, astronauts get FREE TIME to look out the windows, play games, and email friends and family.

30 When British astronaut Tim Peake dialed a wrong number from the ISS phone, a woman on the line assumed it was a PRANK CALL.

31 Circling Earth every 90 minutes, astronauts see 16 SUNRISES AND 16 SUNSETS each day.

35 EVERYDAY FACTS ABOUT

4 Astronauts on the ISS wear T-SHIRTS AND PANTS most of the time, because the temp is kept around 75°F (24°C).

5 The ISS doesn't have a washing machine. Astronauts change their underwear ONLY EVERY OTHER DAY.

6 Astronauts see EXACTLY THE SAME star patterns and constellations that you see on the ground.

7 Due to the MICROGRAVITY in space, most astronauts experience puffy faces, poofy hair, and clogged sinuses.

8 Stuffed-up sinuses make food in space taste much blander than on Earth. Astronauts have found that HOT SAUCE helps.

12 Spacecraft regularly fly to the ISS, bringing CREWS, FOOD, AND SUPPLIES. Up to six spacecraft can visit at one time.

13 The LIVABLE SPACE in the ISS is about equal to that of a 747 airplane. But you share that space with only two to five people.

14 The ISS has two bathrooms, a gym, and a 360-DEGREE WINDOW to see an amazing view of planet Earth and outer space.

15 SPACE TOILETS are not fun. Without strong gravity, how do you keep things you don't want to see again from floating back out? Vacuums!

16 If a space toilet breaks, astronauts need to fix it themselves or use the backup system: DIAPERS.

19 Must-haves in space include TOWELS. They're essential for soaking up any loose liquid that's FLYING AROUND.

20 The space station has SIX PRIVATE BEDROOMS. They're like little closets just large enough to hold one person.

21 If you don't want tools, pencils, clothes, paperwork, or anything else to float away in space, put VELCRO fasteners on it.

22 To sleep, astronauts climb into a SLEEPING BAG fixed to the wall or floor and doze off in any position they can.

Astronaut Karen Nyberg aboard the International Space Station

25 To brush your teeth in space, you can use EDIBLE TOOTHPASTE and swallow it afterward.

26 Astronauts don't shower aboard the ISS. Instead, they take SPONGE BATHS and use dry shampoo to clean their hair.

27 If something is lost on the ISS, check THE VENTS. Items tend to float toward and gather at the AIR INTAKE REGISTERS.

28 When astronauts SWEAT in space, it sticks to their skin in GROSS LITTLE BUBBLES until they towel it off.

32 When astronauts return to Earth from long periods of weightlessness, they may be up to 3 PERCENT TALLER.

33 Astronauts in space need to EXERCISE two hours a day to stay strong for the gravity they'll face back on Earth.

34 Even with exercise, when astronauts return to Earth after several months or more, many are TOO WEAK TO STAND UP.

35 Back on Earth, astronauts must adjust to life in gravity. Sometimes they DROP ITEMS, thinking that they'll just float.

LIVING IN SPACE

1 In 2020, a **car-size asteroid** named 2020 QG missed hitting Earth by only 1,830 miles (2,945 km). It was the **closest near miss of an asteroid** on record.

2020 QG

2 The Gemini 8 spacecraft was **spinning out of control** during its 1966 flight. Command pilot Neil Armstrong took the controls and safely guided the craft back to Earth before he and **his copilot, David Scott, passed out.**

3 Harpoons were supposed to pin the European Space Agency's Philae spacecraft to the surface of tiny comet 67P as it landed. The harpoons failed, and the craft **almost bounced off the comet and back into space.**

4 Ten days before flying past Pluto, **the New Horizons spacecraft went silent.** Scientists fixed the communication problem just in time or their nine-year mission **would have been a total failure.**

5 During the first space walk, Soviet cosmonaut Aleksei Leonov had **trouble getting back into his spacecraft** after his suit greatly inflated. He didn't fit through the air lock! Leonov **had to depressurize his suit** to get inside to safety.

6 In 2019, the European Space Agency had to quickly move its Aeolus satellite out of the way **to avoid running into another dangerously close satellite.**

7 Alan Shepard, the first American in space, was sitting in the rocket on the launchpad, ready to fire, when he told Mission Control, **"I've got to pee."** Instead of stopping the countdown, Mission Control gave Shepard permission to **go in his space suit.**

DANGER IN SPACE

Astronauts Story Musgrave and Jeffrey Hoffman repair the Hubble Space Telescope.

8 In 1969, as the Saturn V rocket carrying the Apollo 12 crew blasted into space, it was struck by lightning—twice. Despite the damage, the spacecraft went on to the moon and then returned the three crewmates safely to Earth.

9 During an eight-hour test in a vacuum chamber, American astronaut Story Musgrave suffered frostbite in his fingers. He recovered and then flew into space to help repair the Hubble Space Telescope.

10 After the Hubble Space Telescope was launched into space, scientists discovered that its mirror was flawed. Images from the telescope were a little blurry. A team of astronauts flew up and repaired it in space.

11 Long after the astronauts left it, NASA's first space station, Skylab, fell to Earth. Pieces of it rained down on Western Australia. No one was hurt by the falling space junk.

12 While on the moon, astronaut Charlie Duke tried to jump as high as he could. He landed on his back and nearly broke his space suit. It held together and Duke made it home safely.

13 During a flight test 14 months before going to the moon, a lunar lander had a problem with its thrusters. Pilot Neil Armstrong ejected and parachuted to safety moments before the craft crashed onto the ground.

14 An explosion on the Apollo 13 spacecraft to the moon caused the astronauts to take emergency actions to swing around the moon and head home. They made it back just before their oxygen supply ran out.

15 Italian astronaut Luca Parmitano nearly drowned inside his space suit during his space walk in 2013. Due to a clogged water filter, cold water started filling his helmet. Parmitano did not panic and made it safely back inside the space station in time.

1 In 1608, a Dutch eyeglass maker named **Hans Lippershey** created a device that allowed people to clearly see distant objects. He is known as the **inventor of the telescope.**

2 The first telescopes could magnify things only three times. Italian scientist **Galileo Galilei** quickly improved upon the designs and made telescopes that **could magnify up to 30 times.**

3 Telescopes like the ones Lippershey and Galileo made use a series of **glass lenses** to gather and magnify light. These are called **refractors** because they **bend,** or refract, the light that comes into them.

4 Telescopes collect light. The **larger the telescope lens or mirror,** the more light it can collect and the better you can see faint and distant objects in space.

5 Polish astronomer Johannes Hevelius built a **150-foot (46-m)-long** telescope that required a crew of assistants to operate.

25 MAGNIFIED FACTS ABOUT

6 The **Cincinnati Observatory** became the first observatory in the world that the public could use when its refracting telescope went into service on April 14, 1845.

7 WHEN A TELESCOPE IS USED FOR THE FIRST TIME, ASTRONOMERS REFER TO THAT MOMENT AS **"FIRST LIGHT."**

8 The **largest refracting telescope** in the world is 40 inches (102 cm) in diameter. It's housed in **the Yerkes Observatory** in Williams Bay, Wisconsin, U.S.A.

9 The **Lowell Observatory** in Flagstaff, Arizona, U.S.A., has several large telescopes open to the public, including the famous telescope that **discovered Pluto.**

10 The **biggest telescope in Asia** is the Vainu Bappu Telescope, located in the South Indian village of **Kavalur.**

11 In 1668, physicist **Isaac Newton** built the first reflecting telescope. Reflectors use **mirrors,** instead of lenses, to capture starlight.

13 In 1845, astronomer William Parsons built a telescope weighing **four tons** (3.6 t). The telescope was so huge it was nicknamed **"the Leviathan of Parsonstown."** (The Leviathan is a huge sea monster.)

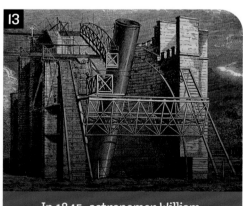

12 In the 18th century, English astronomer **William Herschel** constructed a 20-foot (6-m)-long reflector and then a 40-footer (that's 12 m). They looked like **huge cannons.**

14 In 1948, the 200-inch (508-cm) mirror on the Hale Telescope began scanning the skies from Palomar Mountain, California, U.S.A. It was the largest telescope in the world at the time.

15 The largest telescope in Africa is SALT (the Southern African Large Telescope). It took five years to build and has been observing the skies since 2005.

16 Each of the twin Keck telescopes perched atop Mauna Kea, Hawaii, U.S.A., uses 36 six-sided mirrors that measure 33 feet (10 m) across in total.

17 The Gran Telescopio Canarias located in the Canary Islands is the largest optical telescope in the world. It gathers light with a mirror 34 feet (10.4 m) wide.

18

THE LARGEST TELESCOPES PICK UP SOURCES OF RADIO WAVES WITH LARGE DISHES. THE ARECIBO TELESCOPE USED A 1,001-FOOT (305-M) DISH THAT WAS BUILT INTO A DEPRESSION IN THE MOUNTAINS OF PUERTO RICO.

TELESCOPES ON EARTH

19 The Green Bank Telescope (GBT) in West Virginia, U.S.A., is the largest movable object on land. Weighing about 8,500 tons (7,711 t), this radio telescope can point to almost any object in space that is visible from the United States.

20 Located near Socorro, New Mexico, U.S.A., the Very Large Array is a group of 27 massive radio telescopes. They can be arranged in different patterns and connected electronically to map different parts of the universe.

21 Some telescopes specialize in studying the sun. The McMath-Pierce solar telescope atop Kitt Peak in Arizona is the world's largest solar observatory.

22 Under the football stadium at the University of Arizona is the Richard F. Caris Mirror Lab. There, scientists are building seven 26-foot (8-m)-wide mirrors to install in the Giant Magellan Telescope.

23 The 33-foot (10-m)-wide South Pole Telescope studies light from the earliest part of the universe. It is the largest telescope in Antarctica.

24 CHILE HOSTS SOME OF THE BEST TELESCOPES ON EARTH AT THE LA SILLA PARANAL OBSERVATORY.

25 Astronomers are building the Large Synoptic Survey Telescope (LSST) in Chile. The giant telescope and its camera will be able to take pictures of the entire sky twice a week.

1 Telescopes in space often get **clearer views of the universe** than telescopes on the ground. They never have to worry about clouds or the effects of Earth's atmosphere, and they can see light in different ways.

2  In 1968, NASA launched the Orbiting Astronomical Observatory, the **very first space telescope.**

3 The space shuttle *Discovery* ferried the first major optical telescope, **the Hubble Space Telescope** (HST), into orbit around Earth in 1990.

4 THE HST USES **A MIRROR EIGHT FEET (2.4 M) WIDE.** IT CAN COLLECT MORE THAN 40,000 TIMES MORE LIGHT THAN **THE HUMAN EYE.**

5 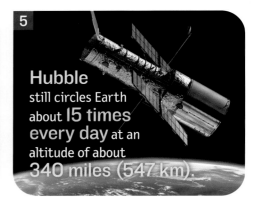 **Hubble** still circles Earth about **15 times every day** at an altitude of about **340 miles (547 km).**

25 FARSIGHTED FACTS ABOUT

6 Astronomers have used the HST to make **1.4 million** observations. This led to more than **17,000 scientific papers** written about astronomy, making the telescope among the most productive scientific instruments in history.

7 The HST produces **amazing, colorful images of deep-space objects.** Many of these astronomical images are edited before you see them to bring out contrast, faint structures, and individual elements and gases.

8 Space telescopes are **hard to fix** and upgrade. It takes tremendous efforts to send astronauts to repair them if they are broken.

10 The **Giotto spacecraft** studied two comets up close. It passed within 400 miles (644 km) of **Halley's comet** and then came within 120 miles (193 km) of comet **Grigg-Skjellerup.**

11 The Infrared Astronomical Satellite (IRAS) had a **special infrared telescope** that could see more than the human eye. It mapped **20,000 galaxies,** 130,000 stars, and 90,000 other objects in space.

9  The European Space Agency's **Hipparcos satellite** measured the distances to stars. It showed how the **Milky Way is changing shape** over time.

12 The **Uhuru satellite,** launched from Kenya in 1970, was the first space telescope to **study x-rays** coming from objects outside our solar system.

13 Between 2003 and 2013, NASA's **Galaxy Evolution Explorer** (GALEX) telescope observed the universe's ultraviolet light. It discovered things not visible to the eye, such as **a black hole eating a star.**

14 In 2013, the **Kepler space telescope** lost its ability to aim accurately at objects. Even though it was millions of miles away, **engineers on Earth reprogrammed it** and were able to keep it searching for exoplanets.

15 The Transiting Exoplanet Survey Satellite (TESS), launched in 2018, has expanded Kepler's work. It is **looking for alien planets** passing in front of distant stars.

16 From 2003 to 2020, NASA's **Spitzer Space Telescope** studied **how our universe is expanding.** It also collected light from exoplanets, comets, and stars.

17 THE HERSCHEL SPACE TELESCOPE, LAUNCHED BY THE EUROPEAN SPACE AGENCY, **STUDIED THE FORMATION OF STARS** AND HOW ENTIRE GALAXIES CHANGE OVER TIME.

18 The Wilkinson Microwave Anisotropy Probe (WMAP) **helped map out the farthest energy in the universe.** It showed that the universe began more than **13 billion years ago.**

TELESCOPES IN SPACE

19 The Japan Aerospace Exploration Agency (JAXA) launched the **Hinode mission** into space to study the sun's magnetic field. It may help scientists understand the sun's explosive surface.

20 Canada's Near-Earth Object Surveillance Satellite (NEOSSat) scans the solar system in search of **any asteroid that may come close to Earth.**

21

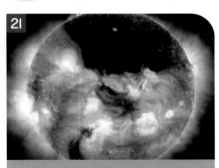

The **Solar and Heliospheric Observatory** (SOHO) is one of the longest-running space telescopes. SOHO has been **watching the sun** and noting its changes almost every day since its launch in 1995.

23 The SOLAR DYNAMICS OBSERVATORY, launched in 2010, takes detailed images of the sun every 0.75 seconds. These pictures have been strung together into **long movies of the sun's activities.**

22 Images taken by the two Solar TErrestrial RElations Observatory (STEREO) telescopes allow astronomers to **see the sun in great detail** from different angles. In fact, their pictures are perfect for viewing with **3D glasses.**

24 The JAMES WEBB SPACE TELESCOPE (JWST), launched in 2021, is the largest telescope ever sent into space. It CIRCLES THE SUN one million miles (1.6 million km) from Earth.

25

The JWST uses a series of six-sided mirrors as it gathers light to peer into the distant universe. It is about **100 times more powerful than the Hubble Space Telescope.**

15 POWERFUL FACTS

1 When an asteroid or meteorite crashes into a planet or moon with tremendous force, it creates an **impact crater—** a huge hole.

2 The largest impact crater on Earth is **Vredefort dome** in South Africa. The hole in the ground is more than 185 miles (298 km) across— **about as wide as the U.S. state of Alabama.**

3 When a huge asteroid created **Chicxulub** (CHICK-soo-loob) **Crater** near Mexico **65 million years ago,** it left a hole more than **100 miles (161 km) wide.**

4 The Chicxulub impact shot so much dirt into the air that it **changed the temperature of the planet.** This probably killed off many species of animals on Earth, including the non-bird dinosaurs.

5 The **Manicouagan Crater** in Québec, Canada, was caused by an asteroid impact 214 million years ago. The crater is 62 miles (100 km) wide and its edges are now filled in with water **making a near-circular lake.**

6 One of the youngest known craters on Earth is **Kamil Crater in Egypt.** Researchers found it by **studying pictures of Earth taken by satellites.**

7 About 50,000 years ago an asteroid 150 feet (46 m) wide crashed into the desert in Arizona, U.S.A. It left **Meteor Crater,** the best preserved impact crater on Earth.

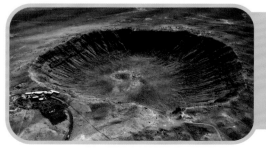

ABOUT GREAT HITS

8 An object more than 60 miles (97 km) across slammed into Mercury almost four billion years ago, creating the planet's largest crater, Caloris Basin. From above, it looks like a bull's-eye made of rings of rock.

9 Astronomers have seen asteroids hitting Jupiter six times since 2009. They show up as little dark splotches for a brief time on the cloud tops.

10 Jupiter's icy moon Europa has an impact crater named Pwyll. The asteroid that created it left cracks on the surface 600 miles (966 km) long.

11 Hyperion, one of Saturn's moons, is so covered in craters that it looks like a sponge. It is so hollow that it would float in water.

12 An object struck Saturn's moon Mimas with such force that it almost tore the moon apart. It left a large crater on one side with cracks going through the tiny moon.

13 On June 30, 1908, a meteor exploded above the ground over Russia. Known as the Tunguska event, the blast flattened trees over an area of 830 square miles (2,150 sq km).

14 In 2016, a comet traveling more than one million miles an hour (1.6 million km/h) got too close to the sun and was swallowed up.

15 In 2009, two small asteroids collided in the asteroid belt. The Hubble Space Telescope captured several pictures of the aftermath, including a lot of dust and debris.

Mercury's Caloris Basin

1 People with **exceptional eyesight** can see the moons of Jupiter, the phases of Venus, and more stars in the sky **without a telescope** than the average stargazer.

2 You don't need a telescope to go sky-watching. Binoculars let you see distant objects like the moon, star clusters, and comets better than the eyes alone.

3 Stars are still in the sky during the daytime. You just cannot see them because the sun is so bright that it washes out the fainter starlight.

4 The human eye can see only one small part of light coming from objects in the universe. This is called visible light.

5 Cameras attached to telescopes can see things the eye cannot. Taking pictures of objects in space is called astrophotography.

6 New General Catalogue (NGC) objects include some of the best and brightest sights in the night sky. Several of them are visible through backyard telescopes.

7 A faint ring of gases curves around the constellation Orion. Called Barnard's Loop, this glowing semicircle can only be seen through astrophotography.

8 When you look at the stars of NGC 457 through a telescope, the stars make an owl or bat shape. This star cluster is nicknamed the Owl cluster or Bat cluster.

SEARCHING THE SKY

The Milky Way

9 With a small telescope, you can find **a little group of stars** in the constellation Vulpecula (Fox) that looks like a **coat hanger.**

10 If you live in the Northern Hemisphere, there are some stars in the southern sky you can never see. People in the Southern Hemisphere can observe those stars but cannot see some northern stars.

11 You can see **two huge star clusters** in the constellation Perseus with a smaller telescope. They are called the **Double cluster** and are 7,500 light-years from Earth.

12 One of the reddest stars in the sky is called La Superba. It changes its brightness so much that sometimes you can see it with the naked eye and sometimes you cannot.

13 Scientists who study galaxies and large parts of the universe believe most of it is invisible to us. They call this invisible stuff **dark matter and dark energy.**

14 Dark matter and dark energy combine to make up about 95 percent of everything in the universe. Only 5 percent of the universe can be seen in telescopes.

15 Many scientists believe there are **multiple universes** or even infinite numbers of universes that we cannot see.

Volcanic eruption on Réunion Island

1 A volcano is **a hole in a planet or moon** where hotter material from the inside erupts out onto the surface or into the air.

2 Four worlds in the solar system have active volcanoes (those currently erupting or that have erupted in human history): Earth, Jupiter's moon Io, Neptune's moon Triton, and Saturn's moon Enceladus.

3 On the Big Island of Hawaii, U.S.A., is Mauna Loa, the largest active volcano on Earth. It is 5.5 miles (9 km) high, but more than **half of it is underwater.**

4 Under the Pacific Ocean lies Tamu Massif, a volcano so large it would cover the entire U.S. state of New Mexico.

5 Yellowstone National Park in the United States sits over an extremely volcanic area. Three eruptions in the distant past created a crater 30 by 45 miles (48 by 72 km) across.

6 The Tharsis region on Mars has 12 massive inactive volcanoes. The biggest are Olympus Mons, Ascraeus Mons, Pavonis Mons, and Arsia Mons. They are up to 100 times larger than any volcanoes on Earth.

7 Sapas Mons, an extinct volcano on Venus, has two peaks. It is 2.5 miles (4 km) tall and surrounded by old lava flows and landslides.

VOLCANO WORLDS

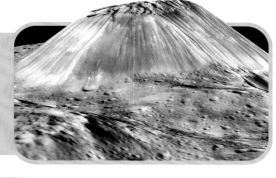

8 Jupiter's moon Io has a sea of lava named Loki Patera, which is about a million times larger than average lava lakes on Earth.

9 Io is the most volcanic place in the solar system. Every day, hundreds of volcanoes on Io are actively erupting.

10 Cryovolcanoes shoot out liquids and ices made of water, methane, ammonia, and chlorine instead of lava. The eruptions form mountains of ice.

11 Ahuna Mons is a cryovolcano on the dwarf planet Ceres. It grew from eruptions of mud and salty water that froze on the surface.

12 Cryovolcanoes on Titan, Saturn's largest moon, spurt gases into the already thick atmosphere.

13 Jupiter's moon Europa is covered in ice. However, geysers gush material, including water, through cracks in the surface.

14 Saturn's moon Enceladus has geysers of water that shoot into space. As the moon circles Saturn, those frozen droplets form a ring around the planet.

15 Triton, Neptune's largest moon, is volcanically active. Its volcanoes spew gases over this otherwise frozen world.

1 During sunrise or sunset, if you look to the opposite side of the sky from the sun, you will see a faint shadow above the horizon. That is Earth's shadow.

2 When sunlight hits a lot of ice crystals in our sky, the sun seems to have a ring around it. This is called a sun halo.

3 SUN DOGS ARE TINY PIECES OF A SUN HALO. THEY LOOK LIKE LITTLE BITS OF RAINBOW TO THE LEFT OR RIGHT OF THE SUN.

4 Just before sunset, the top of the sun can turn an eerie shade of neon green. This rare sight is called the green flash.

5 During a crescent moon, you can often see the dark part of the moon, too. This happens when sunlight bounces off Earth—its "earthshine"—and brightens the moon a little.

6 Meteor showers happen when Earth passes through tiny leftover pieces of comets and asteroids. As they burn up in our atmosphere, these pieces create "shooting stars."

7 Most meteors are the size of a grain of sand.

8 During a good meteor shower, you can see up to 100 streaks of light an hour.

9 Meteor showers happen every year on about the same day. The Perseids peak every August 12–13 and the Leonids on November 17–18.

10 The meteors from the Geminid meteor shower every December are made of parts from asteroid 3200 Phaethon.

11 Really bright meteors are called fireballs. They can glow all sorts of colors, including white, blue, and green, and can break up into many pieces.

12 On October 9, 1992, a meteorite (a rock from a meteor) fell from the sky in the eastern United States and struck a car.

13 On February 15, 2013, a huge meteor streaked across the sky over Chelyabinsk, Russia. For a moment it shone brighter than the sun before it exploded above the ground.

14 The largest meteorite on Earth is in Namibia. Called the Hoba meteorite, it's estimated to weigh 66 tons (60 t).

15 Auroras (also called northern lights and southern lights) happen when gases collide and release colored lights that appear to dance in the sky.

16 Intense solar storms called coronal mass ejections shoot solar material through space. When some of this material slams into Earth, it creates auroras.

17 EARTH IS PROTECTED BY AN INVISIBLE MAGNETIC FIELD THAT BLOCKS MOST OF THE SUN'S PARTICLES, WHILE LETTING IN SUNLIGHT.

18 Auroras in the Northern Hemisphere happen more frequently above Canada, Scandinavia, Russia, and Alaska, U.S.A. These are called the aurora borealis.

19 Auroras that pop up around the Antarctic Circle and can be seen in Patagonia, South Africa, and Australia are called the aurora australis.

20 Auroras can range from a subtle green glow to white and red streaks or to curtains of blue light.

21 IN MARCH 1989, ONE OF THE LARGEST SUNSPOTS ON RECORD SENT A BLAST OF ENERGY TOWARD EARTH. IT CREATED AURORAS THAT WERE VISIBLE FROM CANADA TO CENTRAL AMERICA.

22 In 1859, the sun produced the biggest solar storms to hit Earth's magnetic field. This "Carrington event" created auroras over large parts of the globe.

23 The last time northern lights were visible across a large part of the United States was in November 2001, after a huge sun storm reached Earth.

24 From Earth you can see Mercury, Venus, Mars, Jupiter, and Saturn with the naked eye at different times of the year.

25 On rare occasions, Mercury and Venus pass between Earth and the sun. These passages are called transits.

26 During transits of Mercury and Venus, each planet looks like a tiny black dot in front of the giant sun.

27 A transit of Mercury happens about 13 times every century. The next one will occur on November 13, 2032.

28 Transits of Venus are incredibly rare. The next one won't happen until December 11, 2117.

29 If you are on Mars on November 10, 2084, you could see a transit of Earth. That is when our planet will pass between Mars and the sun.

30 When a planet and our moon (or two or more planets) appear exceptionally close to each other, astronomers call that a conjunction.

31 Venus and Jupiter are in conjunction about once a year. But the next really close conjunction won't happen until 2039.

32 JUPITER AND SATURN COME INTO CONJUNCTION ABOUT EVERY 20 YEARS.

33 The next time all five of the naked-eye planets will share one portion of the sky will be in 2040.

34 The moon regularly follows a path that crosses the stars in the zodiac constellations. It also comes close to the five naked-eye planets.

35 Over a year, the sun follows roughly the same route the moon completes in a month. Astronomers call this path the ecliptic because that is where eclipses can take place.

Aurora borealis

75 FANTASTIC FACTS ABOUT THE COOLEST SIGHTS IN ASTRONOMY

36 A lunar occultation occurs when the much closer moon seems to block out the light of a much farther planet or star.

37 On February 13, 2056, the moon will make a rare double occultation. It will pass in front of Mercury and Mars at the same time.

38 When the moon occults (blocks out) a star, the star's light disappears in a split second. After about an hour, the moon will move away and the star will pop back into view.

39 Four bright stars are close enough to the ecliptic to be occasionally blocked out by the moon: Aldebaran in the Taurus constellation, Regulus in Leo, Spica in Virgo, and Antares in Scorpius.

40 On January 4, 1613, Neptune slipped behind Jupiter in a rare occultation. When it popped back into view that winter, Galileo was watching the sky with his telescope and saw Neptune long before anyone officially discovered it.

41 MARS WILL PASS IN FRONT OF JUPITER ON DECEMBER 2, 2223. THE LAST TIME THIS OCCULTATION HAPPENED WAS IN 1387.

42 Mars looks a lot brighter in the sky when it's close to Earth. The next really close approach for Mars will be on October 6, 2035, when it will be about 39 million miles (63 million km) away.

43 Because most people in the United States live in brightly lit cities or towns, about 80 percent of Americans cannot see the Milky Way (a long band of stars and the bulk of our galaxy).

44 The best way to see the Milky Way is to travel away from cities during a new moon. For best viewing, you can visit dark-sky parks and other places with less light pollution on moonless nights.

45 You can see the Milky Way all year, but some seasons provide better viewing than others. During summer and winter evenings, the Milky Way arches higher in the sky.

46 One part of the Milky Way looks like it broke into two branches with dark sky in between. This is a large area of galactic dust called the Northern Coalsack.

47 THE ZODIACAL LIGHT IS A FAINT PYRAMID-SHAPED REGION OF LIGHT VISIBLE IN THE SKY JUST BEFORE SUNRISE AND JUST AFTER SUNSET.

48 The zodiacal light is caused by sunlight reflecting off trillions of dust particles in the solar system, creating a shimmering glow that can be seen from dark skies.

49 The zodiacal light used to fool late-night stargazers into thinking dawn was about to break, even though daybreak was still hours away. It got the nickname "false dawn."

50 The zodiacal light can also be seen on moonless evenings. To see this "false dusk," look toward the western horizon a few hours after sunset.

51 The gegenschein is an even fainter, ghostly glow in the sky that is rarely seen. It can become visible long after sunset on the opposite side of the sky from the sun.

52 A lunar eclipse happens when Earth passes directly between the sun and moon. Earth blocks the sunlight and casts a shadow onto the moon.

53 Earth actually casts two shadows in space all the time. The sun creates a darker shadow right behind Earth, called the umbra, and a lighter shadow outside the umbra, called the penumbra.

54 A partial lunar eclipse occurs when the sun, Earth, and moon are not aligned precisely enough for the moon to completely enter Earth's shadow. Then, only part of the moon is blocked out.

55 When the moon enters the penumbra, the lighter Earth shadow, it experiences a penumbral lunar eclipse. On a bright full moon, this faint shadow is almost invisible.

56 During a total lunar eclipse, the moon turns gray, orange, pink, and red. This is caused by sunlight bending through Earth's atmosphere, which shifts its color toward red.

57 A total lunar eclipse can be as short as one second and as long as 106 minutes.

58 If you were standing on the moon during a total lunar eclipse, you'd be bathed in red light. When you looked back at Earth, it would be dark and would block out the sun.

59 A lunar eclipse is visible somewhere on Earth about once every 1.5 years. But you must be on the half of Earth facing the moon to actually see it.

60 A solar eclipse occurs when the moon passes between the sun and Earth and casts a shadow onto Earth's surface.

61 LUNAR ECLIPSES HAPPEN ONLY DURING A FULL MOON. SOLAR ECLIPSES TAKE PLACE ONLY DURING A NEW MOON.

62 A partial solar eclipse—when the moon blocks only part of the sun—is the most common type.

63 During some partial solar eclipses, beams of sunlight shine through leaves on trees and make little crescent shapes on the ground like tiny copies of the eclipse.

64 "Totality" is the time when the moon completely blocks the sun during a total solar eclipse.

65 The shadow of a total solar eclipse is generally less than 100 miles (161 km) wide and is visible only from about one percent of Earth's surface.

66 Total solar eclipses are rare events if you don't travel to see them. On average, a spot on Earth is treated to a total solar eclipse about once every 375 years.

67 People who travel to get the best view of eclipses are called eclipse chasers. They go to remote islands and even Antarctica just to glimpse a few minutes of a total eclipse.

68 When the moon is farther from Earth, it will not be big enough to block out the entire sun. This is called an annular eclipse. During an annular eclipse, the sun's edges look like a skinny ring around the moon.

69 ANNULAR ECLIPSES HAPPEN SEVEN OR EIGHT TIMES EVERY DECADE BUT ARE ONLY VISIBLE FROM PART OF THE WORLD.

70 In the moments before and after totality, you can see a sparkle of light around the moon. Astronomers call it the diamond ring.

71 Baily's beads are little balls of sunlight that appear around the edges of the moon. They shine around lunar mountains and through lunar valleys just before a total solar eclipse begins.

72 Unfortunately, total solar eclipses last only a short time. They can be as short as one second and as long as seven minutes and 32 seconds.

73 Because the moon is slowly moving away from Earth, in millions of years it will be too far away to create total solar eclipses.

74 The most eclipses you can see in one calendar year (solar and lunar) are seven. The next time this will happen is in 2038.

75 It's never too early to plan to see the greatest sky show: a total solar eclipse. Mark your calendars to see upcoming ones in Australia on November 25, 2030, and in the U.S. on August 23, 2044.

TIMELINE OF SPACE

Humans have orbited Earth and walked on the moon. They have sent robotic craft to visit all the planets, several moons, and asteroids. These are some of the most important and cool missions to outer space:

October 4, 1957
The Soviet Union launches Sputnik 1. The unpiloted spacecraft becomes the first satellite to circle Earth.

October 7, 1959
The Soviet Union's spacecraft Luna 3 flies around the moon and sends back the first pictures of the moon's far side (something no one on Earth can see).

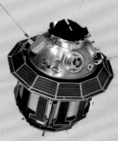

Luna 3

April 12, 1961
Cosmonaut Yuri Gagarin flies aboard the Soviet spacecraft Vostok 1. He becomes the first person to go into space and the first person to orbit Earth.

February 20, 1962
John Glenn pilots the NASA spacecraft Friendship 7 into space and becomes the first American to circle Earth.

June 16, 1963
Cosmonaut Valentina Tereshkova on the Soviet craft Vostok 6 becomes the first woman in space.

March 18, 1965
Cosmonaut Aleksei Leonov performs the first space walk when he exits the Voskhod 2 spacecraft while in orbit around Earth.

Valentina Tereshkova

March 1, 1966
The Soviet Union's Venera 3 spacecraft crashes onto the surface of Venus. Even though it failed to send back any data, it was still the first human-made probe to touch another planet.

December 24, 1968
Jim Lovell, Frank Borman, and William Anders fly around the moon aboard NASA's Apollo 8, becoming the first humans to personally see the far side of the moon and the entire Earth.

July 20, 1969
American astronauts Neil Armstrong and Buzz Aldrin land on the moon during NASA's Apollo 11 mission.

November 13, 1971
NASA's Mariner 9 begins circling the planet Mars and creates the first detailed map of the planet's surface.

December 14, 1972
NASA's Apollo 17 lander rockets astronauts Gene Cernan and Harrison Schmitt off the lunar surface. That mission was the last time humans set foot on the moon.

December 4, 1973
NASA's Pioneer 10 mission makes the first close flyby of the planet Jupiter. Along the way, it is the first spacecraft to fly through the asteroid belt.

July 20, 1976
NASA's Viking 1 lander takes the first pictures from the surface of Mars.

August 20, 1977
NASA launches the Voyager 2 spacecraft. This mission will later fly by Uranus and Neptune.

September 5, 1977
NASA launches Voyager 1 on its journey to visit Jupiter and Saturn.

June 18, 1983
Sally Ride, astronaut and mission specialist on the space shuttle *Challenger*, becomes the first American woman in space.

Voyager 2

February 19, 1986
The Soviet Union begins building the Mir space station. Mir circles Earth until 2001 and is the platform for astronauts to conduct long-term experiments in space.

March 13, 1986
The European Space Agency's Giotto spacecraft flies near the nucleus of Halley's comet in the first close flyby of a comet.

August 25, 1989
NASA's Voyager 2 becomes the first and only mission to fly close to the planet Neptune.

MISSIONS

New Horizons

April 24, 1990
The Hubble Space Telescope is launched. For more than 30 years, this telescope provides some of the best views of our universe.

November 20, 1998
Russia launches the first piece of the International Space Station.

April 28, 2001
American businessman Dennis Tito becomes the first space tourist to purchase a ticket on a rocket that takes him into orbit.

Dennis Tito, at left

January 3, 2004
NASA's Mars exploration rover Spirit touches down on the surface of Mars. A second rover, named Opportunity, lands 21 days later.

July 1, 2004
The NASA and European Space Agency's Cassini mission becomes the first craft to orbit the planet Saturn.

January 14, 2005
The European Space Agency's Huygens probe lands on Titan, Saturn's largest moon.

January 19, 2006
New Horizons, NASA's first ever mission to the dwarf planet Pluto and its moons, launches atop an Atlas 5 rocket from Cape Canaveral, Florida, U.S.A. It flies past Jupiter one year later in what is billed as NASA's fastest mission to date.

November 5, 2007
The Chang'e 1 mission begins orbiting the moon. This Chinese spacecraft maps the lunar surface from very close range before purposefully crashing into the moon.

November 8, 2008
While orbiting the moon, India's Chandrayaan 1 mission discovers water molecules around the moon's north and south poles.

Spirit rover

March 6, 2009
NASA launches the Kepler space telescope. It discovers more than 2,000 exoplanets (planets that orbit distant stars) over nine years in space.

June 13, 2010
After leaving Earth seven years earlier, Japan's Hayabusa mission returns home. It brings back the first samples of an asteroid from its landing on asteroid Itokawa.

March 18, 2011
NASA's MESSENGER mission becomes the first to orbit Mercury. It maps the surface over the next four years.

September 23, 2014
India's Mangalyaan spacecraft (also nicknamed the Mars Orbiter Mission, or MOM for short) starts circling Mars and studying the red planet.

November 12, 2014
The European Space Agency's Philae probe makes the first safe landing on a comet. It bounces several times before finally rolling to a stop on comet 67P/Churyumov–Gerasimenko.

March 6, 2015
NASA's Dawn mission becomes the first spacecraft to orbit a dwarf planet (also the largest asteroid) when it begins circling Ceres.

July 14, 2015
NASA's New Horizons spacecraft flies by the dwarf planet Pluto after leaving Earth nine and a half years earlier.

September 21, 2018
Japan's Hayabusa 2 mission flies around the asteroid Ryugu. It lands two small rovers that begin rolling on the asteroid.

January 1, 2019
NASA's New Horizons mission flies by Arrokoth, the farthest object ever visited by a spacecraft.

January 3, 2019
China's Chang'e 4 robotic probe makes the first landing.

April 19, 2021
NASA's Ingenuity helicopter hovers over the surface of Mars, becoming the first mission to take flight on another planet.

December 25, 2021
The James Webb Telescope launches to study the earliest stars.

MESSIER CATALOG

As a teenager in France, Charles Messier saw a spectacular comet with six tails. This inspired him to become one of the best comet hunters of the 1700s. Messier discovered 13 comets and co-discovered six others. However, Charles Messier is best known today for his list of deep-space objects. In his search for comets, he came across other objects in the sky, including star clusters, galaxies, and nebulae. Messier kept a list of these deep-space objects on his charts. He numbered them M1 (for Messier object #1), M2, and so on. The 110 Messier objects are some of the coolest sights in astronomy. The following are 10 whose photographs are among the most spectacular. (The constellation where they're found is listed in parentheses.)

❶ M1 Crab Nebula (Taurus)

Messier spotted this object while he was looking for Halley's comet's return past Earth. It looked like a little fuzzy star and motivated him to start his catalog. M1 is actually the gas and dust left over from a supernova explosion that lit up the sky in 1054. This supernova was so bright that it could be seen in the daytime.

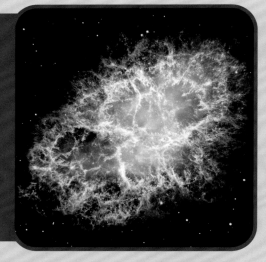

❷ M8 Lagoon Nebula (Sagittarius)

This giant cloud of gas and dust in the Milky Way galaxy is forming new stars. Although not as bright as the Orion Nebula, this region is visible to the naked eye if you're away from city lights. Seen from the dark countryside, it looks like a faint gray cloud in the constellation Sagittarius.

❸ M11 Wild Duck Cluster (Scutum)

M11 is an open star cluster that includes about 2,900 stars roughly 6,200 light-years away from Earth. It is called the Wild Duck cluster because some astronomers thought that the stars looked like ducks flying through space.

❹ M13 Hercules Cluster (Hercules)

This is one of the largest star clusters visible from the Northern Hemisphere. M13 includes about 300,000 stars stretching across almost 150 light-years of our galaxy.

⑤ M16 Eagle Nebula (Serpens)

This star-forming region is named after the clouds of gas that look a little like an eagle's head against the blackness of space. Some space telescope images show M16 in such detail that you can see several newborn stars and pillars of gases that will create many more stars.

⑥ M17 Omega Nebula (Sagittarius)

You can find one of the largest star-forming regions in our galaxy, about 5,500 light-years away. The gases and newborn stars in M17 weigh as much as 30,000 suns. Some of the youngest stars in the Omega Nebula are only about one million years old.

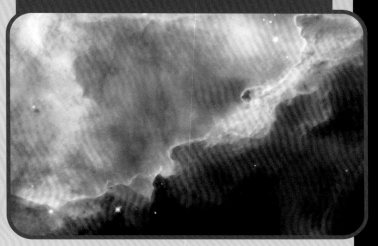

⑦ M20 Trifid Nebula (Sagittarius)

This deep-space object shows off three types of nebulae: an emission nebula (a glowing pink cloud), a reflection nebula (a glowing blue cloud), and a dark nebula (dark streaks of gases in front of clouds).

⑧ M31 Andromeda Galaxy (Andromeda)

M31 is the nearest major galaxy to the Milky Way and has around one trillion stars circling a black hole at its center. It is 2.5 million light-years away, so far that you can barely see it with the naked eye. M31 is getting closer to us and will run into the Milky Way billions of years from now.

⑨ M51 Whirlpool Galaxy (Canes Venatici)

When you see pictures of M51, it looks like a giant spiral galaxy is swallowing up a smaller circular galaxy. This is exactly what's happening! The meeting between the two galaxies has stretched out the spiral arms and started a flurry of star formation as the two galaxies slowly combine.

⑩ M57 Ring Nebula (Lyra)

Through a telescope, the Ring Nebula looks like a little gray smoke ring. However, M57 is an example of a planetary nebula—a shape created when a star ejects its outer gases and turns into a tiny, hot star called a white dwarf. The Ring Nebula is an example of what may happen to our sun at the end of its life (in four to five billion years).

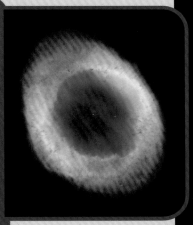

GLOSSARY

asteroid a small rocky object that orbits the sun

asteroid belt the region in the solar system, between the orbits of Mars and Jupiter, where most asteroids circle the sun

Asteroid

astronomical unit (often abbreviated AU) a unit of measurement that is the average distance between Earth and the sun; one AU is equal to 92,955,807 miles (149,597,870 km).

astronomy the field of science that studies objects in space and everything in the universe

atmosphere the gases surrounding a planet, star, or natural satellite

aurora glowing lights in a planet's atmosphere, caused by atoms from the sun moving through the planet's magnetic field; also called the northern lights or southern lights

big bang an enormous explosion that scientists believe was the first event in the formation of the universe

black hole a region of space where gravity is so strong that nothing can escape it, not even light

comet a body of rock, dust, and ice that circles the sun in an elongated orbit

constellation a group of stars that form a recognizable pattern

corona the outermost layer of gases in the sun's atmosphere

cosmology the study of the beginning, end, and structure of the universe

crater a circular hole in the surface of a planet, moon, or other object in space, caused by a meteorite impact or by volcanic action

density a measurement of how much mass an object has within a certain amount of space

diameter the distance through the center of an object from one side to the other; an object's width

dwarf galaxy a galaxy smaller than the Milky Way that holds anywhere from tens of millions to a few billion stars

dwarf planet an object that orbits the sun and is nearly spherical in shape, but has not cleared its orbit like a planet

elliptical galaxy a galaxy that looks like a sphere or ball of stars with no spiral arms

extrasolar planet (also called exoplanet) a planet that orbits a star other than our sun

galaxy an extremely large grouping of stars, gas, and dust bound together by gravity

gas giant a large planet made mostly of gases such as hydrogen and helium

globular cluster a large, densely packed group of stars that has a round or globe-shaped appearance

Globular cluster

gravity the force that pulls objects toward each other; everything with mass has gravity.

habitable zone (also called the Goldilocks zone) the region around a star in which a planet could have liquid water and possibly support life

interstellar existing or traveling between the stars

irregular galaxy a galaxy, typically small, that has no definite shape or features

Kuiper belt the region of the solar system beyond the orbit of Neptune where dwarf planets, comets, and other small objects circle the sun

light-year the distance light travels in a year: 5.88 trillion miles (9.46 trillion km)

lunar eclipse a darkening of the moon that happens when Earth passes between the sun and moon and blocks sunlight from reaching the moon

Lunar eclipse

mass the total quantity of material in an object; an object's mass determines its weight in places with gravity and its resistance to movement.

meteor an object that falls from space and heats up in Earth's atmosphere; a shooting star

meteorite an object that falls from space, survives its plunge through the atmosphere, and lands on Earth

near-Earth object an asteroid or comet whose orbit brings it close to Earth

nebula a glowing interstellar cloud of gas and dust

neutron star a body of densely packed neutrons (tiny subatomic particles) formed after the explosion of a supernova

observatory a building with instruments for studying the sky, such as telescopes

Oort cloud a region of the solar system beyond the Kuiper belt that is the source of comets that orbit far from the sun

open cluster a group of up to a few thousand stars that were formed from the same cloud of gas and dust

orbit the regular path an object in space follows as it revolves around another body

planet a nearly spherical object that circles a star and has cleared its orbit of similarly sized objects

planetary nebula the glowing ring of gas that expands from a star, similar in size to the sun, as it ages

pulsar a neutron star that spins as much as 1,000 times a second, sending out bursts or pulses of energy

Planet Earth

red giant a cool, aging, low-mass star that has expanded greatly from its previous size

revolve to move completely around another object; to orbit

rotate to spin like a top

satellite a natural or human-made object that revolves around a planet or star

solar eclipse a darkening of the sun that happens when the moon passes between Earth and the sun and blocks out some, if not all, of the sun's light from reaching Earth

solar wind a stream of charged particles radiating outward from the sun

spiral galaxy a type of galaxy where the stars and gas appear mainly in curved "arms" and have a spiral or pinwheel shape

star an object in space that fuses elements to create its own light and heat

supergiant a very massive, bright star with a relatively short life span

supernova the sudden and violent explosion at the end of a massive star's life

terrestrial relating to, or similar to, Earth

Supergiant

variable star a star whose brightness changes repeatedly over time

white dwarf the small, dense core of a once larger star

INDEX

Kepler space telescope

Space shuttle

Earth's moon

INDEX

Mariner 10

RESOURCES

Check out the following books and online resources. They will bring you closer to the planets and stars and guide you through the human history of discovering space.

Books

Aguilar, David. *Space Encyclopedia: A Tour of Our Solar System and Beyond*, 2nd ed. National Geographic Kids, 2020.

Aldrin, Buzz, and Marianne Dyson. *Welcome to Mars: Making a Home on the Red Planet*. National Geographic Kids, 2015.

Anderson, Amy, and Brian Anderson. *Space Dictionary for Kids: The Everything Guide for Kids Who Love Space*. Routledge Press, 2016.

Becker, Helaine. *Everything Space: Blast Off for a Universe of Photos, Facts, and Fun!* National Geographic Kids, 2015.

Driscoll, Michael. *A Child's Introduction to the Night Sky: The Story of Stars, Planets, and Constellations—and How You Can Find Them in the Sky*, Rev. ed. Black Dog & Leventhal Publishers, 2019.

Galat, Joan. *Absolute Expert: Space*. National Geographic Kids, 2020.

Johnson, Kelsey. *Constellations for Kids: An Easy Guide to Discovering the Stars*. Rockridge Press, 2020.

Regas, Dean. *100 Things to See in the Night Sky*, Expanded ed. Adams Media, 2020.

Regas, Dean. *Facts From Space!* Adams Media, 2016.

Schneider, Howard. *Ultimate Explorer Field Guide: Night Sky*. National Geographic Kids, 2016.

Tyson, Neil deGrasse. *Startalk: With Neil deGrasse Tyson*, Young Readers Ed. National Geographic Kids, 2018.

Online Resources

A note for parents and teachers: For more information on this topic, you can explore these websites with your young readers:

American Museum of Natural History "Ology: Astronomy for Kids"

Hubble Site "Hubble Space Telescope"

NASA "Galaxies"

NASA "Missions"

NASA "Solar System: Planets Overview"

NASA "Space Place"

NASA "Spot the Station" (guide to seeing the International Space Station)

NASA "StarChild: A Learning Center for Young Astronomers"

National Geographic Kids "Passport to Space"

Sea and Sky "Messier Catalog of Deep Sky Objects"

ThePlanets.org

Time and Date "Astronomy Calendar"

DEAN REGAS has been the astronomer at the Cincinnati Observatory since 2000. He is an educator, author, national popularizer of astronomy, and an expert in observational astronomy. Right now, Dean is probably preparing to observe the next eclipse.

CREDITS

Since 1888, the National Geographic Society has funded more than 14,000 research, conservation, education, and storytelling projects around the world. National Geographic Partners distributes a portion of the funds it receives from your purchase to National Geographic Society to support programs including the conservation of animals and their habitats. To learn more, visit natgeo.com/info.

For more information, visit nationalgeographic.com, call 1-877-873-6846, or write to the following address:

National Geographic Partners, LLC
1145 17th Street NW
Washington, DC 20036-4688 U.S.A.

For librarians and teachers: nationalgeographic.com/books/librarians-and-educators

More for kids from National Geographic: natgeokids.com

National Geographic Kids magazine inspires children to explore their world with fun yet educational articles on animals, science, nature, and more. Using fresh storytelling and amazing photography, *Nat Geo Kids* shows kids ages 6 to 14 the fascinating truth about the world—and why they should care. **natgeo.com/subscribe**

For rights or permissions inquiries, please contact National Geographic Books Subsidiary Rights: bookrights@natgeo.com

Cover designed by Brett Challos

Acknowledgments
The publisher wishes to thank the Potomac Global Media Team: Kevin Mulroy, publisher; Barbara Brownell Grogan, project manager; Patricia Daniels, editor; Carol Norton, designer; Mary Ann Price, photo editor; Heather McElwain, copy editor; and Timothy Griffin, indexer; and the National Geographic Kids Books team: Shelby Lees, senior editor; Brett Challos, art director; Sarah J. Mock, senior photo editor; Molly Reid, production editor; and Anne LeongSon and Gus Tello, production designers.

Hardcover ISBN: 978-1-4263-7342-8
Reinforced library binding ISBN: 978-1-4263-7389-3

Printed in China
23/RRDH/2